TAKUNDA AARON CHIMUTASHU (ZEN ISA)

DOCIE-WARRIOR

Your 10 Day Guide To Becoming A Documentary Filmmaker

Contents

Foreword

The journey that has led me to this point has been perilous and wildly unpredictable. My initial foray into filmmaking must have seemed like a logic-defying endeavor to onlookers. A young man with a BSc in Mechatronic Engineering venturing into what is hardly a lucrative career can't have made much sense to anyone outside of a very small circle. African film-makers of my time will know intimately the difficulties that come with the path of the filmmaker, let alone the path of the documentarian. It is with those struggles and difficulties in mind that I have written this book.

Picking up this book means you now have access to the wealth of knowledge that I gained through blood, sweat, and tears on my journey to becoming a documentary filmmaker. No budding artist should have to suffer the perils of lacking knowledge when they are surrounded by fellow, slightly more seasoned artists. Now, to be clear, I am not claiming to be a perfect filmmaker or even the best; I am merely a man who has chosen to give his suffering meaning by letting it serve those who shall rise up behind him, and possibly grow far beyond him. The journey won't suddenly be easy, but it sure will be **easier** with the practical insights this book provides.

Now, let's dive into it and begin your journey to becoming a mighty **Docie Warrior.**

Acknowledgement

I extend my deepest gratitude to everyone who contributed to the realization of this project. Your support and encouragement have been invaluable.

A special thank you to Amanda for her unwavering belief in me and her patience during the countless hours spent writing and editing. Your love and support have been my anchor.

I am grateful to my friends and colleagues who provided valuable input and encouragement. Your diverse perspectives enriched the content and made this book stronger.

Finally, I want to express my gratitude to the readers. Your interest in this book is a source of motivation, and I hope the insights within these pages resonate with you.

Thank you all for being a part of this incredible journey.

1

DAY 1

Welcome to Solo Storytelling: Your Documentary Filmmaking Journey

Gather 'round, growing warriors of the storytelling savanna! Hear the drums of destiny beat, feel the fire of creativity simmer in your bellies, for we embark on a ten-day hunt for the soul of a documentary! No dusty classrooms or tame tales here, only the raw, pulsating rhythm of ancient filmmaking warrior wisdom, guiding you to forge your own cinematic spear and slay any narrative beast in your path.

These ten days won't be a stroll through sun-dappled meadows. We'll traverse the rugged pre-production plains, wrestling pre-shoot jitters and conquering obstacles with cunning and grit. We'll learn to move like shadows through the interview jungle, capturing stories woven in whispers , and then stitch them together under the starlit skylight of the editing hut.

No ivory towers for us, friends! We'll dance with the spirits of griots, learning the ancient art of weaving truth and emotion into tapestries that captivate hearts and ignite minds. We'll shed the skin of mere filmmakers and emerge as storytellers cloaked in the power of those who walked this path before us, ready to share the untold tales of heroes whispered in the wind.

We will start this journey by diving deep into the nature of "The Documentary". Short lessons with research based exercises will make up your initial studies. These quick enhancements of your sacred knowledge will then give way to longer more practical training, which will take you from being a mere filmmaking citizen, to a full fledged Docie Warrior!

By the time the sun dips below the horizon on day ten, you won't be just another filmmaker; you'll be a griot with a lens, a warrior armed with the power to make audiences gasp, weep, and rise with fists pumping to the rhythm of your narrative . You'll hold within your grasp the embers of a story that can spark a revolution, ignite understanding, and paint the world anew.

So, grab your notebook (or maybe a scrap of animal hide, if you're feeling inspired by our theme), your camera (your spear?), and to claim your story. Remember, this is your hunt, your story to tell, your cinematic fire to tend.

Film on, brave storytellers, film on! And know this, the world, with ears strained and hearts pounding, awaits the tales you'll unleash.

Day 1: Deconstructing Documentary Styles (Deep Dive)

Let's begin by exploring the diverse tapestry of documentary styles, each a unique lens through which we can tell powerful stories and engage audiences.

1. Expository Powerhouse: EXPOSITORY STYLE

Introducing the Expository Powerhouse - think of it as your savvy guide leading you through an amazing adventure of knowledge and wonder. You might have encountered it in shows that unwrap mysteries and explore the world. Let's unravel how this style works, keeping it clear and straightforward!

NARRATION: Envision this: Instead of dull lectures, the Expository Powerhouse narrator is a master storyteller. Picture a voice that's as engaging as your favorite podcast host, making facts come alive. It's about turning information into compelling narratives, where every word feels like a discovery.

VISUALLY STUNNING EVIDENCE: Yet, it's not just about words. This style demands visuals that captivate. Imagine incredible animations revealing scientific processes, striking graphics simplifying complex concepts, or well-crafted illustrations bringing ideas to life. These visuals aren't just for show; they're the proof, making the narrative tangible and taking you places you've never been.

THE SOUNDTRACK: Now, here comes the music, setting the mood for the entire journey. A thoughtfully chosen soundtrack can turn a good documentary into an emotional experience. Think of it like a background harmony, subtly influencing your feelings and enhancing your connection to the content. It's that missing piece that completes the educational puzzle.

CRAFTING THE MASTERPIECE: But it's not a simple mix-and-match of facts and images. The Expository Powerhouse thrives on meticulous editing. It involves seamless transitions, strategic pacing to maintain engagement, and a clear structure that ensures every piece of information lands effectively. It's about finding that sweet spot between education and entertainment, ensuring you're both learning and enjoying the ride.

Lets rehash this section by going through some signs you're watching an Expository Documentary:

- **Compelling Narrator:** If the narrator's voice is as engaging as your favorite podcast host, you've likely stumbled upon an Expository Powerhouse.
- **Striking Visuals:** If the visuals are captivating, using animations, graphics, and illustrations to simplify complex concepts, you're in the right documentary.
- **Emotive Soundtrack:** If the music subtly influences your feelings, turning the documentary into an emotional experience, it's a hallmark of an Expository Powerhouse.
- **Smooth Story Flow:** If the documentary seamlessly guides you from one topic to another, creating a cohesive narrative, then you've found it.

2. Fly-on-the-Wall Intimacy: OBSERVATIONAL STYLE

Ever wondered about a behind-the-scenes look into authentic, unscripted moments of life? Step into the world of observational style documentaries, where cameras become like invisible companions, capturing genuine moments without interference, creating narratives that feel personal, unfiltered, and profoundly moving.

THE UNSEEN CAMERA: In this style, the camera is not a spotlight; it's a fly on the wall, a silent observer that blends into the background. No interviews, no staged scenes - just an unobtrusive lens allowing stories to unfold naturally. Imagine a documentary capturing the quiet details of a family's daily life or an exploration of a community's untold stories. These filmmakers become invisible, letting real moments surface, unfiltered and unrehearsed.

CHARACTERS, NOT SUBJECTS: Observational style isn't about treating people like lab rats. Here, our main characters are not subjects; they're real, with complex lives playing out naturally. Picture witnessing the highs, lows, and vulnerabilities of individuals without judgment. It's about building trust, entering private worlds, and capturing life as it is, flaws and all

MINIMALISM UNLEASHED: In this fly-on-the-wall world, less is often more. Narration steps back, allowing visuals and sounds to tell the story. No dramatic scores; just the hum of daily life, the whispers of conversations, and the unspoken emotions in a passing glance. Imagine a documentary where the power of observation creates its narrative, free from commentary or artificial enhancements.

CRAFTING INTIMACY: Yet, capturing raw moments is just the beginning. Editing plays a vital role in shaping the Observational Style. It's about finding the rhythm of real lives, stitching together moments that reveal deeper truths and unexpected connections. Consider how a documentary turns seemingly ordinary scenes into a powerful portrayal of a community's collective experiences. It's about creating a genuine tapestry, using editing to enhance emotional impact without sacrificing the raw essence of reality.

And here's how to recognize this type of documentary:

- **Invisible Camera:** If it feels like the camera is part of the scene, quietly capturing real moments without interference.
- **Real Characters:** If the people in the documentary seem like real individuals, not actors or subjects under a microscope.
- **Natural Sounds:** If you hear daily life sounds, conversations, and emotions rather than a dramatic soundtrack.
- **Raw Moments:** If the documentary feels unscripted, revealing genuine, unfiltered moments of life.

3. Participatory Perspectives: PARTICIPATORY STYLE

Imagine documentaries where the filmmaker's involvement shapes the narrative, challenging viewers' perspectives. Let's explore how this approach injects personal experiences and sparks conversations about the art of documentary filmmaking itself.

THE FILMMAKER AS THE PROTAGONIST: In this style, the camera isn't just a recording device; it's a companion on a personal journey. The filmmaker becomes the main character, shaping the story through their choices and emotional responses. Whether facing the consequences of a unique experiment or conquering personal fears, the audience witnesses the filmmaker's transformation firsthand, forging a powerful emotional connection.

BLURRING BOUNDARIES: This style disrupts documentary norms. Objectivity takes a backseat as the filmmaker actively influences the story, sometimes becoming part of it. Imagine thought-provoking interviews or playful manipulation challenging viewers to question the filmmaker's role and engage critically with potential biases.

ETHICS ON A TIGHTROPE: With great power comes great responsibility. This style demands deep ethical considerations. How far should a filmmaker influence the story? Is it okay to manipulate events for a compelling narrative? These questions become central, sparking discussions about truthfulness and the filmmaker's responsibility towards subjects and audience.

THE INNER JOURNEY: Capturing a personal, participatory narrative requires careful editing. It's about weaving the filmmaker's experiences with external events, revealing internal struggles and emotional transformations alongside the unfolding story. Imagine intercutting interviews with archival footage, creating a suspenseful narrative around personal risk-taking. It's about crafting a journey that resonates, allowing viewers to share the filmmaker's internal world while grappling with bigger questions raised by the experience.

And here's how to recognize this type of documentary:

- **Filmmaker as Protagonist:** If the filmmaker is actively part of the story, shaping it through their experiences.
- **Blurred Boundaries:** If objectivity takes a backseat, and the filmmaker becomes part of the narrative fabric.
- **Ethical Dilemmas:** If the documentary sparks discussions about truthfulness and the filmmaker's responsibilities.
- **Inner Journey:** If the narrative weaves the filmmaker's personal experiences, struggles, and transformations into the larger story.

4. Reflexive Realities: REFLEXIVE STYLE

Gear up for a mind-bending cinematic journey that'll make your brain dance! Ever caught wind of films that exemplify the Reflexive style? In this unique film approach, filmmakers don't just tell stories; they weave a narrative where they become both the architects and participants. Unlike conventional filmmaking, Reflexive films thrust the filmmaker into the spotlight, acknowledging their presence, gaze, and editing choices. It's as if the director steps out from behind the camera, directly addressing the audience, and dissecting how their filmmaking tools shape the story being told. Imagine a movie where the storyteller is not just an observer but an active player, adding layers of complexity that invite viewers to question whose perspective they're really seeing and who holds the paintbrush crafting the tale. This style brings self-awareness, introspection, and a critical lens to storytelling, challenging traditional conventions in the process.

So, how does this mind-bending magic work? Let's crack open the shell of the Reflexive Style:

THE UNSEEN HAND BECOMES VISIBLE: In Reflexive films, filmmakers aren't concealed directors; they're the architects of the tale. No hiding in the shadows; they step into the light and say, "Hey, I'm here, and here's how I'm crafting the narrative." Picture a movie where the director talks to you directly or showcases how their choices impact the people they're capturing. It's akin to watching a painting come to life, leaving you to question who's truly pulling the strings.

MIRROR ON THE WALL: Reflexive movies don't merely wield the camera; they also turn it inward. It's like a movie examining itself in the mirror. Filmmakers engage in a self-debate within the film, questioning the ethics of their craft. This turns us, the audience, into the judges, determining if the filmmakers are playing fair or playing tricks.

DECONSTRUCTING THE ART OF FILM: These films are rebels breaking free from conventional norms. No straight-line storytelling or pretending to be neutral. Imagine a movie blending reality and fiction or employing intricate interview techniques. It's akin to peeking behind the curtain of a magic show, discovering the secrets, and engaging in conversations about what's genuine and what's movie magic.

THE TWISTED LENS: Editing is the unsung hero in Reflexive films. Jump cuts, voiceovers, and live commentary during the film are tools for dissecting the filmmaking process and revealing its impact on the story. Imagine seamless blending of interviews with footage, making us feel emotions while also exposing the artifice of movie-making. It's like navigating a maze of questions and surprises; you might feel a bit disoriented, but that's part of the adventure!

And here's how you can spot this type of documentary:

- **Direct Communication:** Look for direct filmmaker-to-audience communication.
- **The Film Demystified:** Check if the film delves into its own making, offering a behind-the-scenes peek.
- **Mind Bending:** If the narrative feels like a rollercoaster ride, full of twists and turns, it might be Reflexive.
- **Complex Edits:** Keep an eye out for savvy editing that prompts you to ponder what's real and what's movie magic.

5. Poetic Expressions: POETIC STYLE

Documentaries are not just about facts; they can be like beautiful paintings brought to life through film. Imagine stepping into a world where pictures, dreams, and stories blend together, creating something magical. That's the enchanting realm of poetic documentaries. Let's take a closer look at how filmmakers use visual magic, dreamy storytelling, and emotions to make these cinematic poems.

THE IMAGERY: Picture the scenes in these documentaries as brushstrokes on a canvas. It's like an artist using colors to tell a story, but here, filmmakers use visuals. Imagine a documentary about the environment, where scenes of lush greenery and clear blue skies represent the beauty of nature, and suddenly, dark clouds and pollution-filled scenes signify the challenges our planet faces. Every picture becomes like a secret code, telling a story beyond what words can say.

WELCOME TO DREAMLAND: In poetic documentaries, time doesn't follow a straight line. Memories can feel like dreams, and reality can twist and turn. Picture a documentary exploring a person's life, where childhood memories float into adulthood scenes without a clear order. It's like jumping into different parts of a story, just like how we remember bits of a tale out of order. It's like going on an emotional rollercoaster instead of following a boring timeline.

A SYMPHONY OF SOUNDSCAPES: Sound in these documentaries isn't just background noise – it's a star of the show. Imagine a documentary about a bustling city, where the sounds of traffic, people chatting, and street musicians create a vibrant cityscape. Or picture a nature documentary where the gentle rustling of leaves and the chirping of birds form a serene soundscape. The sounds are like a magical orchestra, playing with our feelings and making the movies even more enchanting.

THE CANVAS OF EMOTION: Editing in poetic documentaries is like creating a beautiful dance. Pictures move, sounds mix, and sometimes, there's silence that makes us feel something deep. Think of a documentary about overcoming challenges, where powerful moments are not rushed but linger, allowing the audience to connect emotionally. It's all about taking us on a journey of feelings – wonder, sadness, or deep thinking.

How to recognize a poetic documentary:

- **Visual Brushstrokes:** Look for scenes where the visuals feel like they're telling a hidden story. It's like each shot is a puzzle piece forming a bigger picture.
- **Dreamy Storytelling:** If the movie makes time feel jumbled, memories like dreams, or blurs reality and imagination, it might be a poetic documentary.
- **Magical Soundscapes:** Pay attention to how the sounds make you feel. Are they more than just background noise? Can you close your eyes and still understand the story through the sounds?
- **Emotional Dance:** If the editing feels like it moves you through different emotions seamlessly whilst keep you slightly off center and visually fascinated by unrealistic imagery, you might be watching a poetic documentary.

6. Interactive Engagements: INTERACTIVE STYLE

The future of documentaries is here! We'll dive into the exciting world of interactive documentaries and virtual reality experiences, where the lines between filmmaker and audience blur. Imagine documentaries where you're not just sitting back and watching but jumping right into the action, where you become part of the story.

ENTER A NEW WORLD: Ever heard of a documentary that takes you on a journey to the bottom of the ocean or to outer space? It's like a movie, but instead of just watching, you can wear special goggles that take you right into the middle of the story. Imagine standing in a deep-sea exploration submarine or floating in the vastness of space—you're not just seeing it; you're feeling like you're really there!

THE VANISHING WALL: The old-style documentary screen is gone! With virtual reality, you're not just a spectator; you're an explorer. Its not just the scenery that you get to experience, you are right in the middle of the action too. Imagine being in a documentary about dinosaurs, and suddenly you're walking next to them, feeling the ground shake—it makes you feel connected to the creatures and events in the documentary, almost like you're experiencing it firsthand.

THE CHOICE IS YOURS: Usually, documentaries have a set story, right? But not here! With interactive documentaries, you get to be the boss. Imagine a documentary about a mystery where you can choose which clues to follow, which rooms to search, and even decide who to interview. Your choices affect how the mystery unfolds, making you feel like a detective in your own movie!

BEYOND VISUAL SPECTACLE: Sure, the engaging visuals in virtual reality are awesome, but these documentaries are about more than just looking pretty. They still need a good story that tugs at your heart and keeps you interested. . It's like using fancy tech to make the storytelling even better!

An Interactive Odyssey: Making one of these documentaries is like crafting a video game. The people behind it have to plan everything perfectly so that it feels like a real adventure. Imagine a documentary about space exploration where you get to choose which planets to visit, and each choice leads to a different part of the story. It's all about making something that grabs your attention, keeps you exploring, and leaves a big impression.

Recognizing an Interactive Documentary:

- **Virtual Reality (VR):** This technology may require special goggles that transport you into a three-dimensional space, enhancing the documentary experience by making you feel physically present in the story.
- **You Make the Choices:** In interactive documentaries, you are not a passive observer but an active participant steering the course of the narrative.
- **Not Just Eye Candy:** While the visual allure of virtual reality is undeniable, interactive documentaries prioritize substance by offering more than just eye-catching visuals.
- **Feels Like You're There:** The hallmark of an interactive documentary is its ability to make you feel like an integral part of the story. It goes beyond passive viewing; it's an immersive journey where you're not merely watching events unfold, but actively participating in them.

***

As we conclude this chapter, fellow Docie-warriors, we've embarked on a captivating journey through the expansive world of documentary filmmaking. Our exploration has illuminated the distinct and nuanced styles—Expository, Observational, Reflexive, Poetic, Participatory, and Interactive—that shape the diverse narratives within this realm.

Remember, dear warriors, these styles are not rigid categories but versatile tools in your cinematic arsenal. The choice of style becomes a deliberate strategy in your quest to make an impact.

With the knowledge of these documentary styles, consider yourself equipped for the battles ahead. Your chosen style is your armor, and your storytelling prowess is the spear that pierces through complexities. Let your voice echo, not just as a documentary filmmaker, but as a Docie-warrior whose stories resonate, inform, and inspire.

Exercise:

Lets tackle the first of many exercises we shall be using to sharpen your spear, intrepid warrior. At the end of each day you will be tasked with trying a task that will enhance your understanding of the topics we would have covered. Lets start with something simple.

1. Look at your top 5 favorite documentaries and, without peaking, try to classify them into the styles we learned about today.

2

DAY 2

Choosing Your Weapon - Matching Styles to Messages

Welcome back, budding Docie Warrior! Yesterday, we learned all about the different documentary styles, understanding each as a unique lens through which narratives unfold. Today, our compass directs us toward a mission of utmost importance: aligning these styles with the messages you wish to convey.

Picture this session as a workshop where the essence of your message combines with the artistic expression of your chosen style, giving rise to a narrative that not only engages, but transforms. It's akin to forging a weapon—shaping each element with precision to create a tool that cuts through the noise and leaves an indelible mark.

With every revelation and insight shared today, envision your documentary taking form, growing into a powerful means of not just storytelling but also influencing hearts and minds.

Navigating the Spectrum: A Deeper Dive into Documentary Styles and Communication Goals

Imagine the documentary world as a vast, vibrant landscape, where different styles bloom like diverse ecosystems, each equipped to handle distinct communication goals. Delving deeper into this terrain, we can explore how these styles flourish in specific environments:

Informing and Educating: The Expository Mountain Range:
Think of expository documentaries as towering mountains, their slopes lined with well-organized facts and insights. Expert narration acts as a seasoned guide, leading viewers through dense information with clarity and purpose. Think of documentaries where complex feats are deconstructed and explained, leaving viewers both informed and awestruck. Most documentaries that follow the stories and lives of animals in the wild are expository.

Raising Awareness and Sparking Action: The Wild Rivers of Participation and Reflexivity:
Here, the waters run wild, carrying viewers into the heart of social injustice and environmental challenges. Participatory documentaries, put the audience face-to-face with the issue,

inviting them to participate in the narrative and witness first-hand the struggles and triumphs of everyday people. Reflexive documentaries, on the other hand, are like mirrors, reflecting on the very act of filmmaking and its impact on the subject matter. Reflexive films challenge viewers to question their relationship with entertainment and animal welfare.

Evoking Emotions and Creating Empathy: The Serene Lakes of Observation and Poetry:

Like still, reflective lakes, observational and poetic documentaries offer profound beauty and intimacy. Imagine a documentary where the camera becomes a silent observer, capturing the subtle realities the relationship between two relatives living in isolation. Or similarly imagine a documentary the follows nature, but without a narrator, using breathtaking visuals and hypnotic music to evoke a sense of awe and connection to the natural world. These styles tap into human emotions, generating understanding and a deep sense of shared humanity.

Entertaining and Engaging: The Trickling Springs of Humor and Suspense:

Even the driest desert needs a refreshing oasis. Entertainment, injected like life-giving water, keeps audiences captivated and invested in the journey. Humor can disarm complex topics, while suspense builds anticipation and propels the narrative forward.

Beyond the Borders: Hybrid Ecosystems and Cross-Pollination:

So why this strange metaphor? Landscapes? Really?

Yeah, really. The beauty of landscapes lies in their fluidity. These styles are not islands unto themselves. Expository documentaries can incorporate emotional storytelling, while participatory films might employ poetic imagery. This cross-pollination enriches the documentary ecosystem, creating hybrid forms that draw in with different audiences and amplify their impact.

Unifying Style and Message: A Practical Example

For this section, lets imagine we are crafting a documentary about ***climate change***. We will explore each style's approach to give you a clear idea of the advantages a capabilities each styles possesses and how each style might adjust your approach to the same general topic.

The choice of your storytelling approach is just like selecting the appropriate weapon, influencing the outcome of your documentary – whether it is just a surface level observation or a compelling and impactful presentation.

THE EXPOSITORY APPROACH:
Expository style relies on precision and knowledge. Facts become the foundation upon which you will build. Narration, your primary tool for conveying your facts, becomes one of your major focuses in crafting your story.

What facts will you focus on? The rising temperatures, the shifting landscapes, the ripple effect of a warming planet? This approach is for the audience yearning for the intellectual thrill of understanding the complex machinery of the Climate crisis. Show them the evidence, lay bare the data, and ignite their minds with the fire of understanding.

FOCUSING ON FACTS:

The critical question in the expository approach is, "What facts will you highlight?" Will it be the rising global temperatures, the transformative shifts in landscapes, or the far-reaching ripple effects of a warming planet? Precision is key here – your audience seeks the intellectual thrill of comprehending the intricate mechanisms of the climate crisis. This approach is tailored for those hungry for a deep understanding, craving an intellectual engagement with the complex realities of our changing environment.

CONVEYING EVIDENCE AND DATA:

The expository style is about more than just information; it's about evidence and data. Showcasing graphs, charts, and compelling visuals becomes integral. Your aim is to lay bare the raw data, presenting it in a way that not only informs but sparks a profound comprehension of the urgency and complexity of climate change.

IGNITING THE MIND:

As a documentarian employing the expository style, your ultimate goal is to ignite minds with the fire of understanding. Present the facts in a manner that resonates intellectually, leaving your audience not just informed but enlightened. This approach attracts individuals who are drawn to the intellectual challenge of grasping the intricacies of the climate crisis.

Practical Guide:

1. **Choose Your Climate Change Focus:** *Select specific aspects of climate change to highlight. Whether it's rising temperatures, melting ice caps, or the impact on ecosystems, narrow down your focus to make the information more digestible.*
2. **Thorough Research:** *Dive deep into the facts. Collect data from reliable sources, scientific studies, and reports. Ensure that your information is accurate and up-to-date.*
3. **Craft a Clear Narrative:** *Develop a structured and clear narrative. Your narration should guide the audience through the facts seamlessly, helping them connect the dots without overwhelming them.*
4. **Visualize Data Effectively:** *Utilize visuals like graphs, charts, and compelling imagery to enhance your storytelling. Make the data visually engaging and accessible.*
5. **Strike a Balance:** *Balance precision with accessibility. While the goal is to provide in-depth information, ensure that your documentary remains engaging and comprehensible to a broader audience.*
6. **Incorporate Expert Insights:** *Feature experts or authorities in the field to provide additional credibility and context. Their*

insights can add depth to your narrative and further enhance the audience's understanding.

7. **Create Intellectual Engagement:** *Craft your documentary to provoke intellectual engagement. Pose questions, challenge assumptions, and encourage viewers to think critically about the climate crisis.*

8. **Inspire Action:** *Conclude by inspiring action. After presenting the facts, guide your audience towards meaningful steps they can take to address or mitigate the climate crisis. Empower them with knowledge and a sense of responsibility.*

THE OBSERVATIONAL APPROACH :

In the Observational Approach to documentary filmmaking, the focus shifts from a strict reliance on facts to capturing the human narrative. Here, the aim is to become the silent observer, blending into the background to witness the raw impact of the events unfolding.

THE SILENT OBSERVER:

Facts alone may not always stir the soul. The Observational Approach adopts the Fly-on-the-Wall style, allowing you to be the silent observer, the shadow in the undergrowth. This style becomes your camouflage, providing the opportunity to witness events with an unobtrusive lens.

CAPTURING RAW EMOTION:

The Fly-on-the-Wall style enables you to capture the emotional essence of a situation. Focus on the fear etched in a farmer's eyes as crops wither or the resilience radiating from a refugee as they rebuild after a flood. This approach thrives on lingering shots of tear-streaked cheeks and trembling hands, weaving a narrative more potent than any scientific report.

CONNECTING THROUGH HUMAN STORIES:

The Observational Approach is tailored for an audience seeking the emotional core, a gut-wrenching connection that compels them to confront the human cost of the chase. This style goes beyond statistics and scientific analyses, delving into the stories that resonate on a deeply human level.

Practical Guide:

1. **Identify Human Stories:** *Begin by identifying compelling human stories within the broader context of climate change. Look for individuals or communities whose experiences can provide a poignant narrative.*
2. **Establish Trust and Access:** *Building trust is crucial when adopting the Observational Approach. Establish a rapport with your subjects, ensuring they are comfortable with your presence. Gain access to their lives, allowing you to capture authentic moments.*
3. **Embrace Fly-on-the-Wall Technique:** *Embrace the Fly-on-the-Wall technique by minimizing interference. Let events*

unfold naturally, capturing genuine reactions and emotions without imposing your presence on the scene.

4. **Focus on Emotional Impact:** Direct your lens towards moments that convey emotional impact. Capture expressions, reactions, and interactions that reveal the human dimension of climate change – the joy, sorrow, resilience, and vulnerability.

5. **Allow Time for Observation:** Patience is key. Allow sufficient time for observation, letting the camera linger on significant moments. This approach requires a slower pace, allowing the audience to connect with the human stories unfolding.

6. **Craft a Narrative Through Scenes:** Instead of relying solely on narration, build your documentary's narrative through carefully selected observational scenes. Let the visuals and raw emotions tell a story that resonates with viewers.

7. **Utilize Cinematic Techniques:** Experiment with cinematic techniques to enhance the emotional impact. Consider the use of lighting, composition, and sound to create a cinematic experience that elevates the storytelling. Don't worry, later chapters shall dive deeper into cinematic techniques.

8. **Maintain Ethical Sensitivity:** Always prioritize ethical considerations when capturing vulnerable moments. Respect the dignity and privacy of your subjects, ensuring that your documentary brings awareness without exploiting their hardships. Ethics will be explored further in later chapters

9. **Edit Thoughtfully:** During the editing process, carefully select and sequence scenes to maintain a cohesive and emotionally resonant narrative. Pay attention to pacing to ensure that the emotional journey unfolds naturally. We will explore editing further in later chapters

10. **Engage the Audience's Empathy:** Conclude by engaging the

audience's empathy. Allow them to connect with the human stories presented and prompt reflection on the profound impact of climate change on real lives.

THE PARTICIPATORY APPROACH:

The Participatory style in documentary filmmaking presents both a challenge and an opportunity. It calls you to step into the story, to be the filmmaker who immerses themselves in the heart of the melting glaciers, confronts politicians with uncomfortable truths, and takes risks to expose the crisis from within. This approach caters to an audience seeking more than information – they crave action. It's a rallying cry that sparks their own aspirations. Your task is to inspire them through your courage, challenge them with your vulnerability, and demonstrate that they, too, can actively contribute to the fight against climate change.

IMMERSIVE FILMMAKING:

In the participatory approach, you are not just an observer; you are an active participant. Walk the endangered landscapes and be present in the midst of the crisis. Capture the raw emotions and experiences that come with being on the front lines of climate change.

CONFRONTING UNCOMFORTABLE TRUTHS:

Challenge yourself to confront uncomfortable truths. Engage with policymakers, scientists, and individuals directly affected by climate change. Present the harsh realities that demand attention and action. Your documentary should serve as a bold confrontation of the issues at hand.

RISKING IT ALL FOR AUTHENTICITY:

Authenticity is key in the participatory approach. Take risks to expose the crisis authentically. Whether it's facing physical challenges or emotional vulnerability, your willingness to go beyond the surface and share the real impact of climate change creates a powerful connection with your audience.

INSPIRING ACTION THROUGH PERSONAL NARRATIVES:

Your documentary becomes a platform for inspiring action. Share your journey and the journeys of those you encounter. Highlight the courage and resilience of individuals fighting against the crisis. Make your audience feel that they, too, can actively contribute to the cause.

Practical Guide:

1. ***Identify Your Role:*** *Determine your role in the documentary – are you an advocate, an explorer, or a firsthand witness? Define your perspective and purpose within the participatory narrative.*

2. **Connect with Key Players:** *Establish connections with key players in the climate change narrative. Engage with scientists, activists, and individuals directly impacted by the crisis. Their voices and experiences will add depth to your participatory approach.*

3. **Plan Your Immersive Experiences:** *Plan immersive experiences that bring you face-to-face with the impacts of climate change. Whether it's visiting affected communities, witnessing environmental changes, or confronting policymakers, these experiences will be the heart of your documentary.*

4. **Document Personal Transformations:** *Capture your personal transformations and challenges throughout the process. Share moments of vulnerability and growth. This authenticity will resonate with viewers and enhance the impact of your documentary.*

5. **Utilize Personal Narratives:** *Make use of personal narratives to humanize the climate crisis. Share the stories of individuals and communities affected, emphasizing their resilience and determination. Connect the personal to the global.*

6. **Balance Advocacy with Objectivity:** *While advocating for action, maintain objectivity in presenting facts and situations. Let the audience draw their own conclusions from the experiences and information you share.*

7. **Encourage Audience Participation:** *Inspire your audience to take action. Provide clear and tangible steps for viewers to get involved in the fight against climate change. Foster a sense of empowerment and collective responsibility.*

8. **Promote a Call to Action:** *Conclude your documentary with a compelling call to action. Encourage viewers to not only be informed but to actively participate in initiatives or movements dedicated to addressing climate change.*

THE REFLEXIVE APPROACH

The Reflexive approach in documentary filmmaking invites introspection and self-awareness. It urges you, the filmmaker, to turn the lens inward, becoming a critical part of the narrative. In the context of a climate change documentary, this style challenges you to reflect on the filmmaking process itself, exploring the impact of your presence on the storytelling. The reflexive approach engages audiences seeking a thoughtful examination of the filmmaking process and the personal connection between the filmmaker and the climate crisis.

FILMMAKER AS SUBJECT:

In the reflexive approach, you are not just behind the camera; you become a subject of the documentary. Consider how your perceptions, biases, and emotions influence the storytelling. Reflect on your role as a storyteller amidst the unfolding climate crisis.

INTERWEAVING PERSONAL NARRATIVES:

Intertwine personal narratives with the broader climate change narrative. Share your thoughts, doubts, and evolving perspectives as a filmmaker embedded in the environmental discourse. This layer of reflexivity adds depth and authenticity to the storytelling.

QUESTIONING THE PROCESS:

Challenge the filmmaking process itself. Ask questions about the choices you make – from framing shots to selecting interviewees. Discuss the ethical considerations and potential biases, prompting the audience to reflect on the nature of documentary filmmaking in the context of a complex issue like climate change.

SHIFTING PERSPECTIVES:

Experiment with shifting perspectives within the documentary. Allow the audience to see the climate crisis through different lenses, including your own. This approach prompts viewers to consider multiple viewpoints and encourages a more nuanced understanding of the environmental challenges we face.

AUDIENCE ENGAGEMENT THROUGH REFLECTION:

The reflexive approach engages a specific audience interested in self-awareness and critical examination. These viewers seek a documentary that goes beyond surface-level information, inviting them to reflect on the interplay between the filmmaker, the audience, and the subject matter.

Practical Guide:

1. **Define Your Filmmaker Persona:** *Clearly define your role as a filmmaker within the documentary. Are you an observer, a participant, or both? Establish the boundaries of your pres-*

ence and explore how it evolves throughout the storytelling.

2. **Integrate Personal Reflections:** *Weave personal reflections into the narrative. Share your evolving thoughts, emotions, and insights related to the climate crisis. Consider creating periodic reflection segments that punctuate the documentary, providing insight into your changing perspectives.*

3. **Question Filmmaking Choices:** *Throughout the documentary, openly question and discuss your filmmaking choices. Address ethical considerations, potential biases, and the impact of your decisions on the storytelling. This self-awareness adds an additional layer of authenticity to the documentary.*

4. **Explore Multiple Perspectives:** *Experiment with presenting multiple perspectives within the documentary. Include diverse viewpoints on the climate crisis and its implications. Showcase the complexity of the issue, allowing the audience to engage in critical thinking.*

5. **Encourage Audience Reflection:** *Prompt your audience to reflect on their own perspectives and preconceptions about climate change. Include moments of pause where viewers can consider the role of the filmmaker and their own role in the broader environmental conversation.*

6. **Maintain a Thoughtful Tone:** *Keep a thoughtful and contemplative tone throughout the documentary. Encourage a sense of introspection and engagement with the subject matter. Avoid overt persuasion, letting the reflexive elements speak for themselves.*

7. **Embrace Imperfection:** *Embrace imperfections and uncertainties in the filmmaking process. Allow moments of vulnerability to shine through, acknowledging the inherent challenges of capturing a complex issue like climate change.*

8. **Facilitate Dialogue:** *Conclude your documentary by facili-*

tating a dialogue. Encourage discussions about the reflexive elements introduced, prompting viewers to share their own reflections and insights. Use social media or other platforms to extend the conversation beyond the film.

THE POETIC APPROACH:

In this style, the focus is on creating an emotional and artistic experience rather than a straightforward presentation of facts. Imagine your documentary as a symphony, where visuals, sounds, and emotions harmonize to evoke a profound connection with the environment. This approach appeals to audiences seeking a more profound and visceral understanding of climate change, inviting them to experience the issue on an emotional level.

VISUAL AND EMOTIONAL SYMMETRY:

Embrace the artistic side of filmmaking by focusing on visual and emotional symmetry. Use breathtaking visuals, expressive cinematography, and evocative music to create a sensory experience. Connect the viewers emotionally to the natural world, conveying the beauty and vulnerability of the environment.

METAPHORICAL STORY TELLING:

Employ metaphors and symbolism to convey the impact of climate change. Rather than directly stating facts, use symbolic imagery and poetic language to draw connections between human activities and their consequences on the planet. Allow the audience to interpret and feel the message.

AUDIENCE CONNECTION:

The poetic approach speaks to an audience desiring a more emotional and artistic exploration of climate change. It attracts those who seek to connect with environmental issues on a deeper, more personal level. Through emotional resonance, your documentary has the potential to inspire empathy and a sense of shared responsibility.

Practical Guide:

1. **Define Your Emotional Landscape:** *Identify the emotions you want to evoke throughout your documentary. Consider the spectrum from awe and wonder to concern and urgency. Craft a narrative that takes your audience on an emotional journey.*

2. **Select Visual Metaphors:** *Choose visual metaphors that symbolize climate change impacts. For example, use images of wilting flowers to represent environmental degradation or vibrant landscapes to signify resilience. Allow these metaphors to speak volumes without explicit narration.*

3. **Curate a Cinematic Palette:** *Develop a cinematic palette by selecting visuals that align with the emotional tone of each segment. Use color grading, lighting, and composition to enhance the mood and atmosphere. Create a visual language that resonates with the poetic nature of your storytelling.*

4. **Incorporate Atmospheric Soundscapes:** *Integrate atmospheric soundscapes to complement the visuals. Use ambient sounds of nature, carefully selected music, and minimalistic narration to create an immersive auditory experience. Let the soundscape enhance the emotional impact of each scene.*

5. **Experiment with Editing Rhythms:** *Experiment with editing rhythms to create a poetic flow. Allow sequences to breathe*

and unfold organically, matching the ebb and flow of emotions. Use pacing to build tension, emphasize beauty, or underscore moments of reflection.

6. **Narrate with Poetic Language:** *Craft your narration with poetic language. Instead of straightforward facts, use metaphorical expressions and evocative descriptions. Encourage viewers to interpret the narrative subjectively, adding their own emotional depth to the experience.*

7. **Offer Room for Reflection:** *Provide moments of reflection within your documentary. These pauses allow the audience to absorb the emotional impact and connect with the deeper messages conveyed through your poetic storytelling.*

8. **Conclude with an Emotional Resonance:** *Wrap up your documentary with an emotional resonance. Whether it's a call to action or a reflective conclusion, leave your audience with a lasting emotional imprint that encourages them to contemplate their relationship with the environment.*

THE INTERACTIVE APPROACH:

The Interactive style in documentary filmmaking transforms the viewer from a passive audience member into an active participant. Imagine your climate change documentary not only conveying information but also allowing the audience to engage, explore, and shape the narrative. This approach caters to individuals who seek more than a one-way conversation; they desire a dynamic and participatory experience. Your role, as the documentarian, extends beyond storyteller to curator, guiding the audience through an interactive exploration of the climate crisis.

CREATING A DYNAMIC EXPERIENCE:

In the interactive approach, your documentary becomes an immersive experience, offering choices, exploration, and engagement. Utilize digital platforms, online tools, or even virtual reality to immerse your audience in the complexities of climate change. Imagine allowing them to navigate melting ice caps or choose which aspect of the crisis they want to explore further.

TAILORING INFORMATION TO USER CHOICES:

Unlike traditional documentaries, the interactive style adapts to the audience's choices. For a climate change documentary, this could mean allowing viewers to select specific topics of interest – be it deforestation, rising sea levels, or renewable energy. Tailor the information flow based on their choices, ensuring a personalized and engaging experience.

ENCOURAGING PARTICIPATION:

Encourage your audience to actively participate in the storytelling process. Pose questions, conduct polls, or integrate user-generated content. This creates a sense of community and shared responsibility, fostering a dialogue around climate change.

SHAPING UNDERSTANDING:

Through interactive elements, empower your audience to shape their understanding of the climate crisis. Provide simulations, quizzes, or virtual tours that allow them to see the cause-and-effect relationships. This hands-on approach deepens comprehension and encourages a more profound connection to the subject matter.

Practical Guide:

1. ***Digital Platforms and Tools:*** *Explore digital platforms and tools that facilitate interactivity, such as web-based documentaries, interactive maps, or virtual reality experiences. These technologies allow users to actively engage with the documentary content.*

2. ***Segmented Information:*** *Segment your documentary content into thematic modules. This way, users can choose which aspects of the climate crisis they are most interested in exploring, tailoring their viewing experience based on their preferences.*

3. ***User-Generated Content:*** *Incorporate user-generated content, such as responses to questions, personal climate change experiences, or even solutions they've implemented. This inclusion fosters a sense of community and shared involvement.*

4. ***Simulations and Games:*** *Integrate simulations or interactive games that illustrate the consequences of climate-related decisions. This hands-on approach enables users to see the impact of their choices, promoting a deeper understanding of the interconnected issues.*

5. ***Real-Time Updates:*** *Include real-time updates on climate-related events, providing users with the latest information*

and reinforcing the ongoing nature of the crisis. This feature ensures that the documentary remains current and relevant.

6. **Community Forums:** *Establish online community forums where viewers can discuss the documentary, share insights, and brainstorm collective actions. This fosters a sense of shared responsibility and encourages a more significant impact beyond the viewing experience.*

7. **Encourage Action Steps:** *Use the interactive platform to guide users toward actionable steps. Provide resources, links, or calls to action that empower viewers to contribute to climate change solutions. Transform engagement into tangible impact.*

The Master Tracker:

But a skilled docie warrior knows one weapon isn't enough. Sometimes, you need to weave your tools together. Imagine an Expository narration punctuated by moments of raw intimacy, where a scientist's explanation of rising sea levels is followed by a fisherman's tearful account of losing his livelihood. Or consider a Participatory film where the filmmaker's journey is interspersed with observational footage of communities already battling the consequences. This harmonious blend amplifies the impact, leaving a lasting impression on the audience.

Remember budding docie warrior, the world is watching, waiting for your story to ignite their understanding, stir their emotions, and ultimately, inspire them to join the chase. With the right tools and the right approach, you can turn any topic from a lurking shadow into a powerful narrative, a story that can change the world, one frame at a time.

***

Review:

- **Informing and educating**: Expository documentaries excel at clearly presenting facts and insights, making them ideal for conveying complex issues like global health crises or historical events. Their authoritative narration and structured approach guide viewers through information in a digestible and impactful way.
- **Raising awareness and sparking action**: The participatory and reflexive styles can be potent tools for activism and social change. By directly involving viewers in the narrative or challenging perspectives, these styles can ignite passion, inspire empathy, and motivate action towards social justice or environmental solutions.
- **Evoking emotions and creating empathy**: Observational and poetic documentaries excel at connecting with viewers on an emotional level. By capturing candid moments and weaving evocative imagery, these styles can tell deeply personal stories, humanize complex issues, and build bridges of understanding between diverse communities.
- **Entertaining and engaging**: While information and impact are crucial, engaging audiences is vital for a documentary's success. Interactive Documentaries can be incorporated into any style, enriching the viewing experience and keeping audiences invested in the story.

Case Studies in Style:

Let's analyze how successful documentaries leverage specific styles to deliver their messages:

*   **"March of the Penguins" (Expository)**: Captivating narration and stunning visuals educate viewers about penguin behavior and the challenges of climate change, inspiring environmental action.*

*   **"Super Size Me" (Participatory)**: Morgan Spurlock's personal experiment on fast food consumption showcases the impact on his health, sparking public debate and policy changes around nutrition.*

*   **"When Lambs Become Lions" (Observational)**: a film that focuses on two sides of the coin in the Kenyan elephant poaching crisis. It weaves together the stories of a cunning and silver-tongued ivory dealer and his cousin, a conflicted wildlife ranger.*

*   **"Waking Life" (Poetic)**: Animated sequences and philosophical dialogues explore existential themes, inviting viewers on a mind-bending journey of self-discovery.*

***

Matching styles to messages is not a rigid formula. Don't be afraid to experiment and combine elements from different styles to create your unique voice. Consider your personal storytelling preferences, the resources available to you, and the emotional impact you want to achieve.

Exercise:

1. Identify your documentary's core message and target audience.
2. Analyze successful documentaries related to your topic, identifying the styles they use and their effectiveness in conveying the message.
3. Experiment by writing short descriptions of your documentary in different styles. Which resonates most with your vision and message?
4. Share your ideas and analyses with the community. Get feedback, discuss challenges, and refine your approach to style and message alignment.

Remember, choosing the right weapon is about finding the perfect fit for your story. Experiment, explore, and trust your instincts to craft a documentary that resonates with audiences and delivers your message with power and impact.

3

DAY 3

Crafting a Compelling Concept - Delving Deeper

Welcome to day 3! We're continuing our exploration of crafting a compelling concept, the beating heart of your documentary. Today, we'll delve deeper into providing you with tools and insights to hone your concept into a captivating narrative ready to engage and inspire.

Imagine this session as a crafting workshop where we chisel away the excess, carve intricate details, and breathe life into the essence of your documentary. Each tool in your hands is a brushstroke on the canvas of your vision, and every insight shared is a compass, steering you toward narrative brilliance.

Uncovering the Layers: Refining Your Central Question

Your central question serves as the guiding light for your entire documentary. It's not just a topic; it's a lens through which you'll explore the world, framing your investigation and shaping your audience's understanding. Remember, the best questions are complex, nuanced, and open-ended, inviting exploration and challenging viewers to think critically.

Here are some strategies for refining your central question:

- **Go beyond the surface:** Instead of settling for a generic question like "What is climate change?", ask "How are rising sea levels impacting the lives of coastal communities, and what systemic changes are needed to address this crisis?"
- **Personalize it:** Inject your own perspective and passion. "As a lifelong resident of a coastal town, I want to understand how climate change is reshaping our way of life and tell the stories of resilience and adaptation amidst rising tides."
- **Consider multiple angles:** Explore the multifaceted nature of your topic. "By examining the perspectives of scientists, politicians, activists, and affected communities, my documentary aims to present a holistic picture of climate change and its far-reaching consequences."

Target Audience in Focus:

Understanding your target audience is crucial for crafting a story that resonates. Consider these factors:

- **Age, demographics, and interests:** What are their concerns, what information do they already have, and what kind of storytelling approach will engage them?
- **Prior knowledge and understanding of your topic:** Tailor your explanations and level of detail accordingly. Strike a balance between providing necessary context and avoiding oversimplification.
- **Emotional triggers and engagement points:** What evokes their curiosity, empathy, or outrage? Utilize visuals, narration, and storytelling techniques that connect with their emotions on a deeper level.

Unleash Your Uniqueness: Standing Out from the Crowd

The documentary landscape is vast, so how do you ensure your story stands out? Identify what makes your perspective unique:

- **Personal connection:** Are you bringing a lived experience or insider knowledge to the table? Share your story alongside others, offering firsthand insights and emotional resonance.
- **Unconventional angle:** Approach your topic from a fresh perspective. Maybe you focus on underrepresented voices, explore unexpected consequences, or utilize innovative storytelling techniques to challenge viewer expectations.
- **Creative format:** Consider non-traditional documentary styles like interactive elements, animation, or experimental filmmaking to connect with your audience in a unique and engaging way.

Narrative Arc Essentials:

Your chosen structure will determine how your story unfolds, weaving information, emotions, and suspense to keep viewers captivated. Explore different options:

- Chronological: A classic approach, following the natural timeline of events. Suitable for documentaries tracing historical developments or personal journeys.
- Thematic: Organize your narrative around overarching themes, presenting diverse perspectives and experiences that illustrate the central message.
- Non-linear: Play with time and structure, using flashbacks, juxtapositions, and parallel narratives to create a more dynamic and thought-provoking viewing experience.

Visual Aesthetic that Tells a Story:

Your visuals are not just illustrations; they actively contribute to your narrative. Consider these questions:

What mood and emotions do you want to evoke?
Choose lighting, color palettes, and camera angles that support your story's tone and message. For example, if you want to create a sense of tension or suspense, you can use low-key lighting, dark colors, and high or low angles.

How will you utilize symbolism and metaphor?
Visual elements can add deeper layers of meaning, prompting viewers to interpret and engage with your documentary on a deeper level. To utilize symbolism and metaphor, you need

to think about the visual elements that can add deeper layers of meaning, prompting viewers to interpret and engage with your documentary on a deeper level. For example, you can use objects, animals, or landscapes that represent something else, such as a theme, a character, or a conflict.

What role will archival footage or animation play?

These can enrich your narrative by supplementing your own footage and offering historical context or diverse perspectives. For example, you can use archival footage to show the past events that are relevant to your story, such as news clips, interviews, or home videos. You can also use animation to show the abstract concepts that are hard to capture with live-action, such as emotions, dreams, or fantasies .

∗∗∗

As we conclude this chapter, let the notion linger: crafting a compelling concept is not a straightforward journey but an evolving odyssey of creativity. Embrace the non-linearity of the process, for it is in the twists and turns that your concept takes shape and gains depth.

Don't hesitate to revisit your choices, treating your concept as a living entity that can adapt and grow. Experiment with various approaches, allowing each iteration to illuminate new facets of your storytelling potential. Remember, seeking feedback is not a sign of weakness but a testament to your commitment to excellence.

Expand your creative circle by sharing your concept with trusted friends, family, or fellow docie warriors. Embrace the diversity of perspectives, and let their honest feedback become a compass guiding you toward refinement. The collaborative spirit is a powerful force in shaping ideas into impactful narratives.

Exercise:

1. Craft your central question and refine it, ensuring it's complex, nuanced, and sparks your curiosity.
2. Create a detailed profile of your target audience, outlining their demographics, interests, and expectations from your documentary.
3. Identify what makes your own perspective unique and how you can leverage it to tell a compelling and original story.
4. Choose a narrative arc for your documentary, explaining how it will support your message and engage viewers.
5. Develop a mood board or sketch out visual elements that represent the desired aesthetic for your film. Consider lighting, color, and camera work to convey the desired emotions and message.

Tip: Analyze documentaries whose concepts and storytelling approaches you admire. Identify their target audience, visual style, and unique angles. Deconstruct their techniques and use them as inspiration for your own project. Here are some examples:

- *"Man on Wire" (Philippe Petit's tightrope walk between the Twin Towers): This captivating documentary blends personal narrative, historical context, and suspenseful visuals to engage viewers from diverse backgrounds. It explores themes of risk, determination, and the human spirit, resonating with anyone who has ever dreamt of achieving the impossible.*

- *"Icarus" (Bryan Fogel's doping investigation): This film starts with a personal quest but unravels into a global conspiracy, showcasing the power of investigative journalism and storytelling to expose injustice. It skillfully utilizes unexpected twists and turns to keep viewers on the edge of their seats, reminding us that the truth can be stranger than fiction.*

Additional Resources:

- *International Documentary Association (IDA): https://www.documentary.org/*
- *Independent Filmmaker Project (IFP): https://www.ifp.org/*
- *POV (PBS documentary series): https://www.pbs.org/pov/*
- *Sundance Film Institute: https://www.sundance.org/*

4

DAY 4

Mastering the Craft - Equipping Your Solo Adventure

Greetings, aspiring Docie Warriors! Today unfolds a chapter that will reveal the technical intricacies of solo filmmaking Buckle up, for this session transforms you into a cinematic MacGyver, arming you with the indispensable tools and skills needed for your solitary odyssey.

Yet, before delving into the technical toolkit, let's pause to acknowledge your most potent weapon as a documentarian—empathy. The heartbeat of your filmmaking journey, empathy fuels the connection between you, your subject, and your audience. Together, we'll traverse the ethically nuanced landscape of documentary filmmaking, exploring the delicate balance required to navigate the human stories that unfold before your lens.

Now, envision yourself not just as a filmmaker but as a storyteller armed with empathy, resourcefulness, and adaptability. These are your allies, your guiding lights in the uncharted realms of solo filmmaking. As we unravel the complexities of ethics, let them serve as the compass directing you toward authentic and impactful storytelling.

Ethical Considerations - Navigating the Moral Compass:

Ethical considerations are essential throughout the documentary filmmaking process, and particularly crucial for solo documentarians navigating complex situations without a large support team. Let's delve deeper into ethical considerations for your solo documentary and equip you with the knowledge and principles to navigate your chosen topic with integrity and respect.

Key Ethical Principles for Solo Documentarians:

INFORMED CONSENT: Ensure participants understand the purpose of your film, how their footage will be used, and their right to withdraw consent at any time. Use clear and concise language, and consider written consent forms for added clarity.

Example:

TRUTHFULNESS AND ACCURACY: Strive for fair and balanced representation of your subject matter. Avoid manipulation, sensationalism, or misrepresentation of facts. Present diverse perspectives and ensure your narrative upholds the principles of truthfulness and objectivity.

PRIVACY AND CONFIDENTIALITY: Respect participants' privacy boundaries. Be mindful of filming personal spaces or capturing sensitive information without consent. If confidentiality is promised, uphold it diligently to protect individuals and safeguard their trust.

HARMING NO ONE: Do no harm. Consider the potential consequences of your film on individuals, communities, or the environment. Avoid exploiting vulnerable individuals or exacerbating existing conflicts. Be sensitive to cultural norms and ethical considerations specific to your chosen topic.

TRANSPARENCY AND ATTRIBUTION: Be transparent about your filmmaking process. Acknowledge limitations, sources of information, and potential biases. Give credit to contributors and collaborators fairly and accurately.

Navigating Complex Ethical Dilemmas as a Solo Filmmaker:

BALANCING ACCESS AND ETHICS: Gaining access to certain subjects or locations may involve ethical compromises. Carefully consider the risks and benefits, prioritize participants' well–being, and be prepared to walk away if ethical principles are threatened.

FILMING SENSITIVE TOPICS: Dealing with sensitive themes like trauma, poverty, or conflict requires special consideration. Approach individuals with empathy and respect, prioritize their safety and comfort, and ensure your portrayal is responsible and avoids sensationalism.

REPRESENTING MINORITY GROUPS: Be mindful of potential misrepresentation or perpetuating harmful stereotypes when filming minority groups. Ensure diverse perspectives are included, collaborate with community members, and avoid generalizations that can reinforce harmful narratives.

DEALING WITH POWER IMBALANCES: As a solo filmmaker, you may encounter power imbalances with authorities, institutions, or individuals with greater resources. Maintain your independence, avoid undue pressure, and prioritize ethical principles over potential benefits or compromises.

SEEKING GUIDANCE AND SUPPORT: Solo Filming doesn't mean complete isolation. Don't hesitate to seek guidance from experienced documentarians, ethics experts, or legal professionals when facing complex ethical dilemmas. Collaborate with trusted advisors to ensure your project adheres to ethical filmmaking practices.

Resources for Ethical Solo Documentarians:

- International Documentary Film Festival Amsterdam (IDFA) Ethics Guidelines: Provides a comprehensive framework for ethical documentary filmmaking.
- Society for Professional Journalists (SPJ) Code of Ethics: Offers principles for journalists that can be applied to documentary filmmaking.
- Ethical Filmmaking Collective: A resource hub for filmmakers with discussions on ethical dilemmas and practical tools.
- Local film associations and documentary communities: Connect with experienced filmmakers in your region to discuss specific ethical challenges and share strategies for responsible filmmaking.

Sub-Exercise:

1. Identify potential ethical challenges in your own documentary: Analyze your chosen topic and identify potential areas where ethical considerations may arise. This could involve consent, privacy, representation, or balancing access with ethical principles.
2. Develop an ethical framework for your project: Outline your commitment to informed consent, truthfulness, privacy, and minimizing harm. Consider establishing ground rules for yourself and any collaborators to ensure ethical filmmaking practices are upheld throughout the

process. e.g *"No crew member can ask the subject their name as the subject's identity is a sensitive issue"*

3. Seek feedback and guidance: Discuss your ethical concerns with trusted advisors, peers, or relevant experts. Gaining different perspectives can help you identify potential blind spots and ensure your approach is responsible and well-informed.

4. Document your ethical decisions: Maintain a written record of your decisions regarding consent, access, and representation. This can be helpful for transparency and accountability, especially if your film raises ethical questions in the future.

Remember, ethical filmmaking is an ongoing process that requires careful consideration and continuous learning. By prioritizing ethical principles, seeking guidance, and adapting your approach when necessary, you can navigate the complexities of solo documentary filmmaking with integrity and create a work that contributes positively to the world.

Now, let us look through your arsenal and find out what other mighty tools you must wield on this amazing journey

Your Essential Gear Arsenal

No filmmaker embarks on an adventure without a trusty toolkit. Let's unpack the essentials for your solo mission:

CAMERA: DSLR or Mirrorless cameras offer versatility and quality, while mirrorless options provide lightweight portability. Consider your budget, shooting style, and desired image quality.

LENSES: A versatile zoom lens like a 18-55mm is a good starting point, allowing you to capture wide shots, portraits, and close-ups. Prime lenses offer superior image quality and low-light performance, but require carrying multiples for greater focal range.

*A DSLR or Mirrorless video camera with an interchangeable lens mount is a **powerful** weapon*

SOUND: Capture crystal-clear audio with a dedicated external microphone, like a shotgun mic for interviews or a lavalier mic for on-the-go recording. Invest in a windjammer to minimize outdoor noise.

TRIPOD: For stable shots and time-lapse captures, a lightweight tripod is invaluable. Consider compact travel tripods with ball heads for quick adjustments.

LIGHTING: While natural light is your best friend, consider portable LED lights for indoor filming or low-light situations. Small reflectors can bounce existing light and add warmth to your shots.

BACKUP BATTERIES AND STORAGE: Power outages are the bane of a filmmaker's existence. Double up on batteries and invest in reliable storage cards (SD or CFexpress) to accommodate extensive footage.

Pre-Production Checklist - Your Roadmap to Success:

Preparation is key to a smooth filming process. Utilize this checklist to avoid on-set Panic (templates related to this section can be found in the resources section at the end of this book:

SCRIPT WRITING: Develop a story outline (*see resources*), shot list, and interview questions (if applicable). Storyboards can visualize key scenes and camera angles.

Shot List Columns Explanation:

A shot list is a table that is used to keep track of what shots you need to get in order to shoot your documentary in the style you have chosen. You fill in the shot list in order to organize all your shoots and avoid forgetting to shoot a particular shot and finding out later in post-production.

Shot Number:

- *Purpose:* The shot number provides a unique identifier for each shot in your documentary. It helps maintain a chronological order and aids in organizing the footage during post-production.
- *Usage:* Assign a sequential number to each shot, starting from the beginning of your documentary. This numerical order simplifies the editing process and ensures continuity.

Shot Description:

- *Purpose:* The shot description offers a brief but informative overview of what happens in the shot. It serves as a quick reference for the content and context of each shot.
- *Usage:* Write a concise description that captures the key action, emotion, or information conveyed in the shot. This description assists both during shooting and editing.

Shot Type:

- *Purpose:* The shot type categorizes the visual style or technique used in the shot. It provides insight into the framing and composition of each shot.
- *Usage:* Specify whether the shot is a close-up (CU), medium shot (MS), wide shot (WS), or any other relevant type. This helps in planning a diverse visual narrative and ensures a mix of shot sizes.

Location:

- *Purpose:* The location column indicates where the shot takes place. It helps in coordinating the shoot, ensuring that you are prepared with the necessary equipment for each location.
- *Usage:* Clearly state the physical or thematic location of the shot. This information aids in efficient planning, especially if you are shooting in multiple places.

Camera Angle:

- *Purpose:* The camera angle describes the position of the camera concerning the subject. It influences the viewer's perception and emotional response to the shot.
- *Usage:* Specify whether the camera angle is low, eye-level, or high. Understanding the camera angle helps in conveying the desired mood and perspective.

Camera Movement:

- *Purpose:* The camera movement column outlines any planned camera motion during the shot. It adds dynamism

to the footage and enhances storytelling.
- *Usage:* Indicate if there's a pan, tilt, dolly, zoom, or any other movement planned. This information guides the camera operator and ensures a deliberate and effective visual approach.

LOCATION SCOUTING AND PERMITS: Secure filming locations and obtain necessary permits. Research potential challenges like access restrictions or noise limitations.

SUBJECT RELEASES: Ensure written consent from individuals featured in your documentary. Explain the purpose, usage, and limitations of their participation. *(See Resources)*

EQUIPMENT CHECKLISTS: Double-check your gear, ensuring everything is charged, functioning properly, and packed securely. A small travel kit for cleaning cloths and spare batteries is a lifesaver.

TRAVEL AND LOGISTICS: Plan your filming schedule, transportation, and accommodation. Research local customs and weather conditions to avoid surprises.

CONTINGENCY PLANS: Be prepared for the unexpected. Consider backup locations, alternative solutions for technical issues, and emergency contact information.

Mastering the Technical Terrain: THE CAMERA

Imagine your camera as a symphony for the eyes. Each setting plays a crucial role in composing your visual narrative:

THE BASICS:

- **Aperture:** This, the iris of your lens, controls the "bokeh," that dreamy blur in the background. A wide aperture (low f-number) isolates your subject, emphasizing their presence in bustling environments. A narrow aperture (high f-number) keeps everything sharp, perfect for capturing intricate details in a bustling market scene.
- **Shutter Speed:** The maestro of time, shutter speed dictates how long the shutter stays open, sculpting motion. A fast shutter freezes fleeting moments, capturing a protestor's defiant leap. A slow shutter paints ethereal brushstrokes of light trails, emphasizing the passage of time over a bustling city.
- **ISO:** This versatile performer amplifies the camera's sensitivity to light. Low ISO maintains pristine clarity in daylight interviews, while high ISO lets you delve into dimly lit interiors, capturing the raw authenticity of a backstage conversation.

THE SENSOR AND YOUR LENS: YOUR CAMERA'S EYE

- **Camera Sensor Size:** The camera sensor is a crucial component in digital photography and videography. It is a light-sensitive surface that captures the image projected by the camera lens. The size of the sensor plays a significant role in determining the field of view, depth of field, and overall image quality.

- **Focal Length:** The focal length of a lens is the distance between the lens and the image sensor when the subject is in focus. It is usually measured in millimeters (mm). Focal length determines the magnification and angle of view of a lens. Shorter focal lengths provide a wider field of view, while longer focal lengths offer more magnification and a narrower field of view.
- **Crop Factor:** Crop factor, also known as focal length multiplier, is a numerical value that expresses the difference in size between a camera's sensor and a full-frame sensor (35mm). It affects the effective focal length of a lens when used on a camera with a sensor size smaller than full frame.

FOCUS: GUIDING THE VIEWERS GAZE

Focus is your spotlight, directing the audience's attention. Mastering these techniques ensures your story resonates:

- **Autofocus:** Your trusty companion, autofocus keeps your subjects sharp during dynamic interviews or unexpected moments of action. Choose from modes like single-point for precise control on a speaker's face or continuous for tracking dancers in a cultural celebration.
- **Manual Focus:** Take the director's chair! Manual focus

unlocks a world of creative possibilities. Shift focus subtly from a bustling street to a child's hopeful eyes, drawing the viewer deeper into the scene.

EXPOSURE: PAINTING WITH LIGHT

Exposure is the delicate alchemy of aperture, shutter speed, and ISO, balancing light to create a compelling visual tone. Understanding these controls empowers you to paint your documentary with the right light:

- **Metering:** Your camera's built-in light reader suggests exposure settings. Learn about different modes like spot for highlighting a speaker's face or evaluative for balancing the entire scene at a protest rally.
- **Exposure Triangle:** Imagine a triangle where each corner represents one setting. Tilting the triangle adjusts overall brightness. A wider aperture lets in more light, requiring faster shutter speeds or lower ISO, and vice versa.
- **Histogram:** This visual map of your image's tones reveals if it's under- or overexposed. Learn to interpret its peaks and valleys to fine-tune your exposure for stunning results in challenging lighting conditions.

BEYOND THE TECHNICAL:

Documentary filmmaking is more than just technical virtuosity. It's about capturing the human spirit, the rawness of reality, and the unspoken stories beneath the surface. Remember:

- **Framing:** Compose your shots with intention. A tight close-up on a protestor's fist conveys defiance, while a wide shot

of a refugee camp underscores the vastness of suffering.
- **Movement:** Use camera movement to guide the viewer's emotions. A slow pan across a deserted factory evokes melancholy, while a handheld camera following a protester evokes the chaos of the scene.
- **Depth of Field:** Decide whether to isolate your subject or capture the context. A shallow depth of field throws the background out of focus, drawing attention to a child's tear in a war-torn street. A deep depth of field keeps both the child and the bombed-out buildings sharp, emphasizing the impact of war.

Mastering the Technical Terrain: THE MICROPHONE

Your microphone is your closest confidante in this sonic adventure. Here are some trusty options:

THE BASICS:

- **Lavaliers:** Clip these discreet warriors directly onto your subjects, catching every intimate whisper and emotional tremor. Perfect for interviews and close-up interactions.
- **Shotgun Mics:** Think of them as snipers for sound, honed to focus on your subject's voice while suppressing background noise. Ideal for interviews in dynamic environments.
- **Booms:** Imagine this graceful giant, extending to capture audio from a distance while remaining out of frame. Excellent for capturing ambient sounds and interviews in

flexible settings.

THE ART OF PLACEMENT:

Microphone placement is an intimate dance. Here are some steps to make it a tango worth remembering:

- **Proximity is key:** Get your mic close to the sound source! For interviews, aim for chest level, just off to the side, to avoid plosive pops from "p" and "b" sounds.
- **Mind the background:** Be a noise ninja! Identify and mitigate unwanted sounds like traffic, air conditioners, or distant chatter.
- **Layer your sounds:** Combine different mic types for rich dimensionality. Use a lavalier on your subject while capturing ambient sounds with a boom or recorder.

YOUR EARS ARE YOUR GATEKEEPER

Invest in good headphones! They become your window into the sonic world, revealing muffled voices, rogue wind gusts, and any gremlins hiding in your audio. Monitor your levels like a hawk, adjusting gain on the fly to ensure clean, vibrant recordings.

BEYOND THE GEAR:

- **Levels:** Keep your audio in the "sweet spot," avoiding peaks that crackle and dips that disappear. Monitor those meters like a ship's navigator!
- **Record in WAV:** This uncompressed format preserves pristine audio quality, giving you more flexibility in post-production.

- **Safety net:** Enable a backup recording track at a lower level, catching those unexpected audio drops.

SOLO STRATEGIES:

- **Practice & preparation:** Test your mics and settings before rolling, familiarizing yourself with your equipment and the recording environment.
- **Double duty:** Consider using a camera operator-friendly mic like a shotgun, allowing you to focus on framing while capturing decent audio.
- **Embrace post-production:** Utilize audio editing software to polish your recordings, removing unwanted noise and enhancing clarity.

Mastering the Technical Terrain: THE LIGHTS

Natural light is your ally, bathing your subjects in an authentic glow. Learn to read its nuances:

- **Golden hour magic:** Capture the ethereal hush of dawn or the warm embrace of dusk, when the sun paints landscapes in golden hues and softens shadows.
- **Diffused light:** Embrace overcast skies! They spread light evenly, creating soft, natural-looking illumination perfect for interviews or close-ups.
- **Windows:** Let windows be your stage lights! Position your subject near a window for flattering illumination with soft

shadows. Use diffusion panels to avoid harsh contrasts.

REFLECTORS: BENDING LIGHT TO YOUR WILL

Reflectors become your silent collaborators, manipulating natural light to your advantage:

- **Silver bounce:** A crisp, neutral reflector, ideal for bouncing light into shadows and adding sparkle to a subject's eyes.
- **Gold bounce:** Creates a warmer, softer glow, perfect for emphasizing skin tones and adding a cozy ambiance to interviews.
- **Flags & Gobos:** Control unwanted light, blocking harsh direct sunlight or reducing background distractions. Think of them as light sculptors, shaping the scene to your vision.

THREE POINT HARMONY:

For indoor shots, where natural light might be a fickle friend, master the basic three-point lighting setup:

- **Key light:** Your main spotlight, shaping the scene and directing the viewer's eye. Use softboxes or umbrellas for diffusion, creating flattering shadows.
- **Fill light:** Bathes your subject in softer light, reducing harsh shadows and adding depth. Position opposite the key light, adjusting intensity for balance.
- **Backlight:** Creates separation from the background, adding dimensionality and a subtle rim of light around your subject. Experiment with placement and intensity for dramatic or subtle effects.

SOLO STRATEGIES:

- **Portable lights:** Invest in lightweight LED panels or battery-powered strobes for on-the-go flexibility.
- **Quick setups:** Practice setting up your three-point lighting efficiently, utilizing stands and clamps for rapid deployment.
- **Embrace post-production:** Use color grading software to subtly adjust lighting, enhance the mood, and refine your cinematic vision.

Understanding and utilizing this knowledge is essential to become a documentary filmmaker. This section pretty much gave you an overview of the "What", on Day 6, you will go further and cover more of the "How" and "Why" of utilizing these techniques and equipment.

***

As you embark on this journey of honing your craft, remember that the path to proficiency is paved with experimentation and a willingness to learn from every experience.

Take the time to familiarize yourself with your gear, treating it not just as tools but as extensions of your storytelling prowess. Conducting test shoots in diverse scenarios allows you to explore the capabilities of your equipment, adapting and refining your techniques along the way. Embrace the learning process as an ongoing venture, recognizing that each frame, each challenge, and each mistake contributes to your growth as a solo filmmaker.

Exercise:

1. Develop a pre-production checklist for your specific documentary project, tailoring it to your needs and shooting style.
2. Research an ethical dilemma faced by a documentarian. Discuss potential solutions and the importance of ethical filmmaking practices.
3. Practice basic camera operation and audio recording techniques. Shoot a short scene focusing on lighting and sound quality, evaluating your results and identifying areas for improvement.

Tip: Watch behind-the-scenes documentaries or interviews with solo filmmakers to gain insights into their technical approaches and challenges overcome. Remember, every filmmaker's journey is unique, so embrace your own style and learn from the experiences of others.

5

DAY 5

Assembling Your Toolkit - Mastering the Art of Solo Filmmaking

Today's mission is constructing the very foundation of your filmmaking experience. This isn't just about capturing footage; it's an exploration into the art of assembling a medley of skills, resources, and collaborative prowess to make your film dreams a reality.

Our journey is multifaceted, beginning with the identification and harnessing of resources that will serve as the building blocks of your cinematic endeavor. But we won't stop there; our compass points us towards the creation of your dream team – a collective force of talents and perspectives converging to breathe life into your narrative tapestry.

By the end of this session, you won't merely be equipped with technical know-how; you'll possess the insight to orchestrate a symphony of skills, seamlessly weaving them together to manifest your creative vision.

Resource Inventory:

Before venturing out, let's take stock of your available resources. Having a firm understanding of the resources you have access to from the get-go can be the difference between planning an impossible project with a scope that's too wide for you, and crafting a perfectly executable project that might need a few extra embellishments.

Consider these crucial elements:

BUDGET: Be realistic about your financial limitations. Explore funding options like grants, crowdfunding, or personal investment. Remember, creativity and resourcefulness can go a long way!

1. *Know your story:* Before crunching numbers, solidify your concept! Define your theme, filming locations, interview subjects, and estimated shooting timeline. A clear roadmap saves you from budgetary detours.
2. *List the essentials:* Identify non-negotiables like basic camera equipment (phone? DSLR?), audio recorder, travel costs, and editing software. Research average expenses and factor in contingency funds for unexpected hiccups.
3. *Prioritize ruthlessly:* Is lighting equipment crucial or can natural light work? Can interviews happen remotely

or do you need travel funds? Be honest with yourself, prioritizing needs over wants.

4. *Embrace DIY spirit:* Get creative! Borrow equipment from friends, utilize free resources like libraries and public spaces for filming, and explore open-source editing software. Remember, resourcefulness is a filmmaker's superpower.

EQUIPMENT: Utilize what you already have and prioritize essential gear like camera, audio recording devices, and basic lighting equipment. Rent or borrow additional equipment when necessary.

1. *Match needs, not trends:* Don't chase the latest tech if it doesn't serve your story. A basic, light camera with good stabilization is often better than a huge fancy rig with loads of nic-naks.
2. *Read reviews, consult experts:* Online forums and YouTube channels are bursting with insights from experienced filmmakers. Learn from their wisdom and ask questions before you buy or rent any equipment.
3. *Prioritize user-friendly tools:* Complex interfaces can eat up precious time. Choose equipment that's easy to learn and operate, especially when you're solo.
4. *Versatility is king:* Look for multi-purpose gear that can adapt to different situations. A flexible tripod, a camera with multiple lens options, or a small lighting kit that doubles as on-camera lights can save you money and space.

LOCATION ACCESS: Secure filming locations with proper permits and permissions. Utilize public spaces, community centers, or personal connections when possible.

1. *Align with your theme:* Your location isn't just a pretty backdrop; it should organically weave into your story's fabric. Choose environments that visually echo your theme, reflecting emotions, conflicts, or historical significance. A bustling city might signify urban struggles, while a serene nature reserve could embody hope and resilience.
2. ***Think beyond the obvious:*** Explore hidden gems – local shops, community centers, or unexpected public spaces – that offer unique visual textures and authentic charm. These locations can also open doors to deeper connections with the local community.
3. *Utilize visual storytelling:* Consider lighting, sound, and accessibility. Will warm sunlight bathe your interview in a hopeful glow, or will the harsh shadows of an abandoned building heighten the sense of tension? Does the background noise add ambience or distract from your subject? Think about how the location's sensory experience contributes to your narrative.

Permission Process:

1. *Research is key:* Start by identifying who owns or manages the location. Is it a public park, a private business, or someone's personal property? Each requires different approaches and permissions.
2. *Be professional and courteous:* Always introduce yourself and explain your project clearly. Highlight the positive

impact your documentary can have on the location or community. Remember, you're asking for a favor, so politeness and professionalism go a long way.

3. *Respect private property*: If filming on private land, obtain written permission from the owner. Be clear about your filming dates, equipment needs, and potential disruptions. Offer compensation if relevant, showing your respect for their property and privacy.

4. *Negotiate and compromise:* Be prepared to adapt your plans. If filming at your first-choice location isn't feasible, consider alternatives that still resonate with your vision. Flexibility and a willingness to compromise can go a long way.

5. *Embrace community connections:* Network with local residents, community organizations, or even potential interviewees. Their personal connections and knowledge can open doors to locations you might not have considered, granting you insider access and authentic storytelling opportunities.

TRANSPORTATION: Plan your filming logistics considering budget and accessibility. Public transportation, bicycles, or carpooling can be cost-effective options.

1. *Public Transport:*

Conquering public transport as a solo filmmaker requires smarts and savvy! Plan your journey like a pro using apps like Google Maps and Citymapper, avoiding missed connections and lost adventures. You can save bucks as well by utilizing travel passes if you're a frequent rider, ditching single-ticket woes. That said, patience is your superpower – pack a good book and embrace the occasional travel delay, it's all part of the public transport tango.

Remember though, safety first! Research potential risks like pickpockets and keep your equipment close in a secure bag. Travel light, and if your budget allows, consider equipment insurance for extra peace of mind.

2. *Bicycle:*

Two wheels can take you a long way on your solo documentary journey! While sturdy, reliable bikes are ideal, don't hesitate to explore budget-friendly used options, just prioritize quality for safety's sake. If your adventure is temporary, consider bike rentals or bike-sharing programs – perfect for cities with dedicated cycling paths. And remember, a little DIY goes a long way! Mastering basic bike maintenance like fixing flats or adjusting brakes can save you precious time and money on the road. So, hop on the saddle, embrace the wind in your hair, and let your bike become your trusty steed on your solo docu-odyssey!

3. Carpooling:

Online forums and social media groups are your gateway to carpool companions, both fellow filmmakers and friendly locals. But remember, it's not just hitching a ride – clear communication is key. Talk costs, routes, and schedules upfront to avoid bumpy misunderstandings later. And life throws curveballs, so be flexible and keep the vibes positive. A smooth carpool journey starts with a little prep and a lot of open communication. Happy travels!

Building Your Dream Team:

Alright, so this whole time we have been discussing solo filmmaking, but I had to include this section simply because your career, someday, will go beyond solo. Besides, even when you are riding solo, collaboration can enhance your project so lets consider these potential teammates and contributors:

- **Experts and Advisors:** Seek guidance from individuals with specialized knowledge relevant to your topic. They can provide valuable insights and ensure factual accuracy.
- **Translators and Interpreters:** If filming multilingual individuals, ensure accurate translations for interviews and voiceovers. Consider hiring professional services or utilizing community volunteers.
- **Crew Members:** Depending on your needs and budget, consider recruiting individuals for specific roles like camera assistants, sound technicians, or editors. Remember, clear communication and mutual respect are key for a successful collaborative journey.

How to Collaborate:

- **Barter system:** Offer your skills (editing, graphic design, translation) in exchange for needed resources like equipment, location access, or transportation.
- **Community crowdfunding:** Organize local fundraising events, raffles, or bake sales to generate support within your community.
- **Equipment co-ops or rentals:** Share or rent equipment within your local filmmaking community, reducing indi-

vidual costs and fostering collaboration.

· **In-kind sponsorships:** Approach local businesses for equipment loans, discounted services, or product donations in exchange for promotional mentions or film credits.

Technology also offers a treasure trove of resourceful tools:

The magic of storytelling never fades, but the tools we use to weave our tales are ever-evolving. While the craft of the documentary might date back to flickering silent films, the internet now offers a treasure trove of digital gems to add sparkle to your project.

Research? Forget dusty archives, dive into online databases filled with academic journals, historical documents, and data that speaks volumes. Language barriers crumble with translation apps, letting you capture the stories of diverse voices. Collaboration transcends borders with cloud platforms, where footage sails through the digital breeze, uniting distant editors and filmmakers.

And the visuals?Affordable drone technology grants you an eagle's eye view, while time-lapse tech compresses the very essence of time, adding mesmerizing drama to your scenes. These digital tools aren't shortcuts though, they're paintbrushes on a broader canvas, amplifying the impact of your storytelling.

Embrace the Unconventional:

Beyond the Crew: Unconventional Partnerships to Power Your Docie

Okay, so you're crafting your documentary masterpiece, but the traditional tools and partnerships feel a bit... predictable? Don't beat yourself up, that's your "docie sense" telling you to add a little spice to your already amazing arsenal! There's a vibrant ecosystem of unconventional partnerships waiting to supercharge your project with fresh perspectives, diverse skills, and unexpected magic. Let's delve into the treasure trove of collaboration beyond the usual suspects:

COMMUNITY NAVIGATORS: Filming sensitive topics or venturing into unfamiliar landscapes? Local community liaisons are your secret weapon. Their cultural understanding paves the way for meaningful access, builds trust with hesitant subjects, and unlocks stories hidden from outsiders. Think of them as your cultural bridges, ensuring your narrative resonates with authenticity and respect.

PASSIONATE APPRENTICES: Remember the fire in your belly when you first fell in love with filmmaking? Student interns or volunteers can reignite that flame in your project. Their youthful enthusiasm and eagerness to learn bring fresh energy to the crew, while their diverse skillsets can fill gaps and offer unexpected insights. Don't underestimate the power of mentorship – guide their budding talent, offer real-world experience, and watch your passion multiply tenfold.

SKILL SWAPPING SYNERGIES: Collaboration isn't a one-way street! Fellow filmmakers have a wealth of specialized skills waiting to be tapped. Partner with a sound wizard to elevate your audio landscapes, collaborate with a color grading guru to craft breathtaking visuals, or team up with a graphic design maestro to make your title sequence sing. Barter skills, offer reciprocal support on future projects, and watch your documentary blossom with the combined magic of diverse expertise.

VIRTUAL VISIONARIES: Distance is no barrier in the age of video conferencing! Reach out to experts, academics, or even international interviewees using platforms like Zoom or Skype. Tap into their unique perspectives, expand your geographic reach, and gather invaluable insights without breaking the travel bank. Remember, sometimes the most powerful voices come from unexpected corners of the globe, so embrace the virtual handshake and let technology bridge the physical divide.

Story Telling Enhancements:

While the usual suspects like camera and audio are crucial, don't neglect these often-overlooked resources:

- **Archival footage and photographs:** Add historical context, visual texture, and emotional depth to your narrative. Explore online archives, libraries, or personal collections.
- **Creative commons resources:** Utilize royalty-free music, sound effects, and images to enrich your film without copyright headaches. Platforms like Freesound and Pexels offer a treasure trove of options.
- **Storytelling props and visuals:** Simple objects, symbolic

elements, or handmade visuals can enhance your narration and engage viewers on a deeper level. Get creative and personalize your storytelling tools.

- **Community partnerships:** Tap into local expertise and resources. Libraries, community centers, or cultural organizations can offer filming locations, interview subjects, or volunteers.

***

In this session, we equipped you with the essentials for production - practical tips to turn your documentary dream into real footage. You've learned how to plan your shots, pick the right gear, and even build a dream team of helpers.

Remember, a resourceful documentarian is a powerful filmmaker. Embrace creativity, explore unconventional solutions, and build collaborative partnerships to transform your vision into a remarkable reality. With a resourceful toolkit and the spirit of collaboration, you can conquer limitations and craft a captivating documentary that resonates with audiences and leaves a lasting mark.

Exercise:

1. Identify one area of your production where resources are limited. Brainstorm creative solutions like utilizing alternative resources, collaborating with others, or employing technology to overcome the challenge.
2. Research and compile a list of relevant community or-

ganizations or businesses that could potentially offer partnerships or in-kind support for your documentary.

3. Explore online databases and research tools related to your documentary topic. Discover valuable resources that can enrich your narrative and provide factual backing.

4. Experiment with video conferencing platforms and cloud storage options to envision how you can collaborate with team members or interview subjects remotely.

5. Share your resource optimization strategies and collaboration ideas with the community. Discuss challenges, exchange tips, and learn from each other's resourceful approaches.

Tip: Watch documentaries praised for their innovative resourcefulness. Analyze how they made the most of limited budgets, utilized unconventional partnerships, and leveraged technology to create impactful narratives. Learn from their ingenuity and apply their strategies to your own project.

6

DAY 6

Capturing Compelling Footage - The Practical Art of Solo Filming

Welcome to the pivotal point of your documentary filmmaking odyssey – the moment where theoretical knowledge transforms into the practical wisdom of a seasoned warrior. Having delved into the conceptual and technical intricacies of crafting a documentary, prepare to step onto the sacred grounds of hands-on experience. I recall the first time I decided to grab my first weapon, a Canon 750d, and venture into the ever trying world of documentary filmmaking. It was a testing, but ultimately rewarding ordeal. I jumped in blind, but you won't have to suffer the confusion of directionless exploration. It is time to imbue yourself with the essence of observation, master the essential arts of capturing footage, and embrace the unforeseen moments that weave the tapestry of true storytelling.

Now, stand ready to sharpen your senses, for we venture into the heart of the wilderness, where the art of keen observation becomes a skill that will set you apart. Like an African warrior attuned to every rustle of the leaves and nuance of the wind, you too shall learn to perceive the untold stories that unfold around you.

Observational Prowess: Seeing Beyond the Obvious

A major part of your journey to becoming a Docie-warrior is mastering the art of observation by becoming a silent observer in various settings. A fly on the wall, a leopard in the trees, a lion in the amber grass. As a documentarian, you will need to blend seamlessly into the environment, ensuring minimal disruption, and focus on deciphering human interactions and reactions through subtle body language and facial expressions.

You must develop your capacity to "listen" with your eyes. Pay keen attention to the surrounding soundscape, whether it's the lively hustle of a bustling marketplace, the rhythmic hum of machinery, or the gentle rustle of leaves in the wind. These auditory elements will significantly enhance the depth of your visuals, creating a more immersive and engaging experience for your audience.

In the realm of documentary film making, prioritize the capture of details that effectively convey a compelling story. Seek out objects with symbolic meaning, zoom in on close-ups that reveal the emotions etched on people's faces, and thoughtfully frame elements within the environment that seamlessly contribute to your overarching narrative. Whether it's a weathered hand clutching a worn tool, a photograph marred by the evidence of tears, or a child's innocent drawing adorning a wall – these details, rich in nuance, add layers of meaning to your narrative, allowing it to resonate on a deeper level without the need for explicit verbalization.

In the following section we are going to rehash some technical elements we covered in previous chapters, but with more practical instructions on how to get your image from plain captures, to story telling excellence.

Technique with a Twist:

This section is an expansion on the elements we learned about on Day 4. Feel free to refer to chapter 4 to refresh on any terminology that might seem a little foggy.

FRAMING AND COMPOSITION: Elevate your visual storytelling by embracing unconventional framing and composition. Go beyond the conventional and experiment with leading lines, dynamic compositions, and unconventional angles to create visually captivating shots.

Leading Lines:
Identify and leverage prominent lines in your environment, such as roads, fences, or rivers. Position yourself strategically so that these lines naturally guide towards your subject. Experiment with various angles to optimize the effectiveness of leading lines, resulting in a visually dynamic composition.

Practical Setup: While shooting, consciously position yourself to incorporate the identified leadin

Rule of Thirds:

Utilize the rule of thirds as a foundational principle. Activate the grid (its like a giant hashtag over your image) on your camera or visualize it while framing your shot.

Practical Setup:

Enable the grid on your camera and position your subject at one of the intersecting points. For ca

Negative Space:

Consciously incorporate negative space around your subject, especially above their head (head space). Apply the rule of thirds by placing your subject's eyes on one of the top intersections for a balanced look.

Practical Setup: Mindfully frame your shots, leaving intentional negative space around your subje

Unconventional Angles:

Explore various shooting angles to find what best suits your narrative. Keep your image interesting by using these angles to convey your subjects feelings, mood and situation. Even the slightest changes are subconsciously noticed by your audience and can influence how they digest your frame, subject and story.

Practical Setup: During shooting, physically position yourself for different angles. Experiment with lo

Foreground Elements:

Foreground elements in photography and filmmaking refer to objects, subjects, or elements positioned in the front part of the frame, closest to the camera. These elements are essential for creating a sense of depth and dimension within the composition. They can serve various purposes, such as leading the viewer's eye into the scene, framing the main subject, or adding visual interest and context. Foreground elements are especially effective in enhancing the overall composition and guiding the viewer's attention to specific aspects of the image.

Practical Setup:

Choose a Relevant Foreground Element:

- *Select a foreground element that adds depth, context, or frames the main subject. Consider elem*

Determine Camera Placement:

- *Position your camera to highlight the chosen foreground element. Experiment with different angles (*

Set Aperture for Depth of Field:

- *Choose an aperture setting that allows for a sufficient depth of field. A wider aperture (lower f-numb*

Frame the Shot:

- *Compose the shot by framing the foreground element in a way that complements the overall narrativ*

Consider Lighting:

- *Evaluate the lighting conditions and how they affect the foreground element. Utilize natural or artifi*

Test Focus Points:

- *Use your camera's focus points to ensure the chosen foreground element is sharp and well-defined. A*

Assess Background Composition:

- *While focusing on the foreground, be mindful of the background composition. Ensure that backgroun*

Capture Test Shots:

- *Take test shots to assess the overall composition, focus, and exposure. Review the images to identify (*

Refine and Capture the Shot:

Fine-tune the composition, focus, and exposure based on the test shots. Once satisfied, capture the final

Example:

____

- *Photographing a landscape with a prominent rock or flower in the foreground can lead the viewe*

Background Elements:

Background elements are the components of an image or frame situated behind the main subject or focal point. They provide context, atmosphere, and contribute to the overall visual narrative. Background elements are crucial for setting the scene, establishing the environment, and conveying additional information about the context in which the image or footage is captured. The choice of background can significantly impact the mood and tone of the composition. Well-considered background elements contribute to a balanced and harmonious visual experience, complementing the main subject without overshadowing it.

Practical Setup:

Identify Key Background Elements:

- *Select background elements that directly contribute to the story's atmosphere, mood, or context. Con.*

Determine Camera Placement:

- *Position your camera to include the chosen background elements. Experiment with different angles c*

Set Aperture and Depth of Field:

- *Choose an aperture setting that ensures a suitable depth of field. Consider whether you want the*

Frame the Shot:

- *Compose the shot by framing the main subject with the selected background elements. Ensure a f*

Consider Lighting Conditions:

- *Evaluate the lighting in the scene and how it interacts with the background elements. Adjust you*

Test Focus Points:

- *Use your camera's focus points to ensure both the main subject and background elements are wel*

Assess Foreground Composition:

- *While focusing on the background, be mindful of foreground elements that may complement or e*

Capture Test Shots:

- *Take test shots to review the composition, focus, and exposure. Assess how the background eleme*

Refine and Capture the Shot:

- *Fine-tune the composition, focus, and exposure based on the test shots. Once satisfied, capture th*

THE RELATIONSHIP BETWEEN CAMERA SENSOR SIZE, FO-CAL LENGTH AND CROP FACTOR:

Field of View (FOV):

Larger sensors capture a wider field of view for a given focal length compared to smaller sensors. Full-frame sensors generally have a wider FOV than APS-C sensors, and APS-C sensors have a wider FOV than Micro Four Thirds sensors.

Depth of Field (DOF):

Smaller sensors, due to their inherent crop factor, provide a deeper depth of field for a given aperture and focal length compared to larger sensors. This affects how much of the image is in sharp focus.

Low Light Performance:

Larger sensors typically perform better in low-light conditions because they can capture more light. They have larger individual pixels, which results in better signal-to-noise ratios and improved image quality in low-light situations.

Effects on Full Frame, APS-C, and Micro Four Thirds:

Full Frame: Full-frame sensors offer a wider field of view, shallower depth of field, and better low-light performance. They are commonly used in professional and high-end consumer cameras

Practical Element:

- *Crop Factor: 1x (No crop factor)*

Example: A 50mm lens on a full-frame camera provides the equivalent field of view as a 50mm lens.

APS-C: APS-C sensors are smaller than full frame but larger than Micro Four Thirds. They strike a balance between portability and image quality. APS-C cameras are popular among enthusiasts and some professionals.

Practical Element:

- *Crop Factor: Approximately 1.5x to 1.7x (can vary between manufacturers)*

Example. For a 50mm lens on an APS-C camera with a 1.5x crop factor, the equivalent field of view is

Micro Four Thirds: Micro Four Thirds sensors are the smallest among the three. They are found in more compact and lightweight cameras. While they may sacrifice some low-light performance and depth of field control, they offer portability and versatility.

Practical Calculation:

- *Crop Factor: 2x*

Example: A 50mm lens on a Micro Four Thirds camera has an equivalent field of view of 100mm (50n

All focal lengths mentioned in this book are based on a Full frame sensor. Apply relevant conversions depending on your camera type.

THE ARSENAL OF SHOT TYPES: Now lets delve into the significance of different shot types, breaking down their uses, effects, and practical steps to achieve them. Whether it's the intimate focus of a close-up, the expansive view of a wide shot, or the nuanced storytelling of a medium close-up, each shot type contributes to the overall cinematic experience.

Diverse shot types go beyond mere aesthetics; they are powerful storytelling devices that convey information, emotions, and context. A well-chosen shot can enhance the impact of a pivotal moment, immerse viewers in the setting, or emphasize the subtleties of a character's expression. By mastering the art of shot selection, you will gain the ability to create a dynamic visual language that enriches your storytelling and captivates audiences.

Close-up (CU):

A close-up shot captures a subject in detail, typically framing their face or a specific part of their body. It eliminates surrounding context to focus on specific emotions or details.

Close-ups are effective for conveying emotions, emphasizing facial expressions, and creating a strong connection between the viewer and the subject. They are commonly used in intimate or intense scenes.

Practical Setup:

1. Position the camera close to the subject to emphasize facial features or details.

2. Use a lens with a shorter focal length (35mm or below) to create a more intimate feel.

3. Focus on the eyes, expression, or specific detail you want to highlight.

4. Consider the subject's comfort and maintain a natural, unintrusive shooting distance.

Extreme Close-up (ECU):

An extreme close-up shot zooms in even further than a close-up, capturing very small details such as the eyes, lips, or hands.

ECU shots intensify the focus on minute details, creating a sense of intimacy, tension, or emphasis on a specific object or emotion.

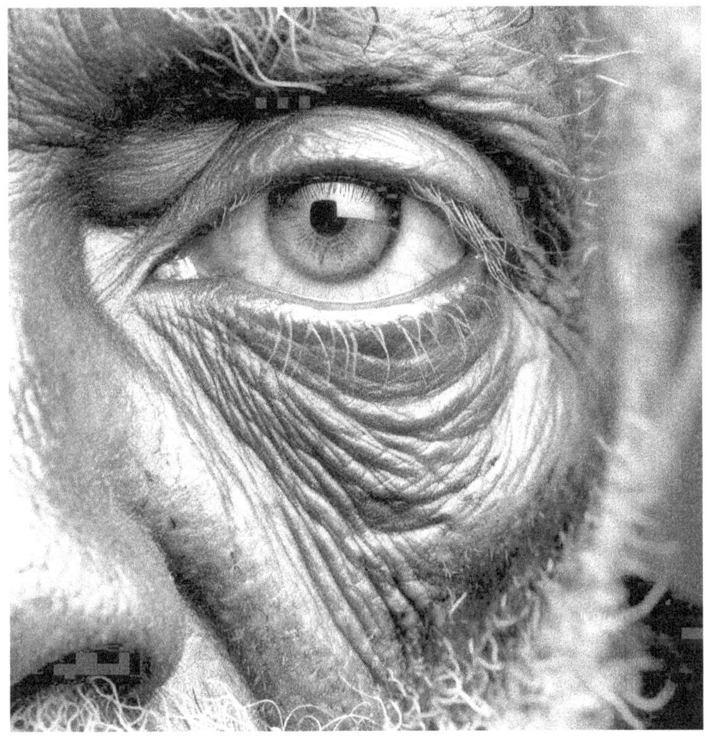

Practical Setup:

1. *Move the camera extremely close to the subject, often within centimeters.*
2. *Utilize a macro lens for extreme detail and focus on small features like eyes, lips, or hands.*

3. *Be mindful of lighting to ensure clear visibility of tiny details.*

4. *Direct the viewer's attention to a specific, meaningful element within the frame.*

Medium Close-up (MCU):

A medium close-up shot frames the subject from the chest or shoulders up, providing more context than a close-up while still highlighting facial expressions.

MCU shots balance intimacy with context, making them suitable for dialogues, reactions, or scenes where body language is crucial.

Practical Setup:

1. *Position the camera at a moderate distance from the subject, typically only showing chest or should*
2. *Use a lens with a focal length between 50mm and 85mm for a balanced perspective.*
3. *Frame the subject's face and upper body, allowing for a clear view of facial expressions.*
4. *Consider the subject's body language and its relevance to the scene.*

Mid Shot (MS):

A mid shot frames the subject from the waist up, providing

a more extensive view than a medium close-up but less detail than a full shot.

MS shots are versatile, suitable for capturing interactions between characters, conveying body language, and maintaining a balanced perspective.

Practical Setup:

1. *Position the camera at a moderate distance from the subject, framing them from the waist up.*

2. *Use a lens with a focal length between 50mm and 85mm for a standard perspective.*

3. *Capture interactions between characters or emphasize body language.*

4. *Maintain a balanced composition to provide a clear view of both the upper body and facial expressic*

Very Wide Shot aka Extreme Wide Shot(VWS/EWS):

A very wide shot, also known as an extreme long shot, captures the subject within the context of their surroundings, often showcasing the entire setting.

VWS shots establish the location, setting, or environment. They are ideal for introducing a new scene or providing a broad visual context.

Practical Setup:

1. *Position the camera at a significant distance from the subject to capture both subject and surrou*

2. *Use a wide-angle lens (24mm or below) for a broad field of view.*

3. *Emphasize the vastness of the environment by showcasing a significant portion of the surround*

4. *Be mindful of composition, ensuring the subject remains visible within the wider frame.*

Wide Shot (WS):

A wide shot frames the subject within their surroundings,

offering a broader view than a mid shot but not as extensive as a very wide shot.

WS shots provide context while maintaining focus on the subject. They are useful for showing interactions between characters within a defined space.

Practical Setup:

1. *Position the camera at a moderate distance from the subject, framing them within their surroundir*

2. *Use a lens with a standard focal length (35mm to 50mm) for a balanced view.*

3. *Convey the subject's interaction with their environment while maintaining focus on the central*

4. *Consider the overall composition, ensuring a balance between the subject and surroundings.*

CAMERA MOVEMENT:

LIGHTING MASTERY: A very wise man once said "artists create with paint, the way cinematographers create with light". Mastering lighting is essential to crafting your creative masterpiece and knowing how to manipulate light is vital to becoming a solid story teller.

On a budget, its best to embrace the power of natural light as your primary source. However, don't shy away from experimenting with shadows, reflections, and other available light sources to evoke specific moods and enhance the atmosphere in your shots. In low-light situations, consider incorporating small LED panels strategically to maintain clarity and visual appeal.

Diffuse Natural Light:

Optimize the softness and flattering qualities of natural light by positioning your subject near windows, doorways, or shaded areas. This diffused lighting minimizes harsh shadows, providing a gentle and even illumination, particularly useful for capturing portraits or scenes with a softer aesthetic.

Practical Setup: Identify areas with soft, indirect natural light. Position your subject in these spaces, ensurin

Bounce Light:

Experiment with bouncing natural light onto your subject using white reflectors or cardboard. This technique fills in shadows, producing a more balanced and well-lit image. Begin by placing the reflector opposite the primary light source, allowing it to bounce light onto your subject's face, especially beneficial in environments with uneven or harsh lighting conditions.

Practical Setup: Position a white reflector or cardboard opposite the primary light source, directing the

Negative Fill:

Introduce the concept of negative fill as you advance in your lighting skills. Strategically minimize light on one side of your subject to create contrast and depth. Achieve this effect by using black flags or any black cloth with a slightly textured surface. Experiment with negative fill to add dimension to your shots, emphasizing contours and textures.

Practical Setup: Position a black flag or cloth opposite the primary light source, casting a shadow on one sid

Using Sheets, Softboxes, etc., for Diffusion:

Expand your lighting toolkit by incorporating tools for con-trolled diffusion. Soften harsh light sources using sheets, softboxes, or diffusers. Whether shooting in direct sunlight or indoor settings, experiment with these tools to distribute light evenly, reducing harsh shadows and providing pleasing illumination for your subjects.

Practical Setup: When shooting in direct sunlight, place a sheer fabric or specialized diffusion material

Golden Hour Magic:

Leverage the enchanting lighting conditions during the golden hour, which occurs during sunrise or sunset. The warm and inviting tones of this natural light add a cinematic touch to your footage. Plan your shoots around these times to capture stunning visuals with a captivating, golden hue that enhances the overall mood of your scenes.

Practical Setup. Plan your shoots during the early morning or late afternoon to take advantage of the golde

Creative Shadows:

Experiment with shadows to add depth and intrigue to your shots. Utilize silhouettes against a bright background to infuse mystery or drama into your visuals. Play with the interplay of light and shadow to create visually compelling compositions that enhance the storytelling aspect of your documentary.

Practical Setup: Identify strong light sources and experiment with positioning your subjects to create ca

AUDIO CLARITY IS KING: Sometimes, the best visuals can be ruined entirely by awful audio. Many times I have stood proud at my achievements where my framing, lighting and visual story telling are concerned, only to be completely blindsided by terrible audio. Bad audio will destroy your audience's immersion and bring their journey with your creative masterpiece to an abrupt and premature end.

To avoid this painful fate, invest in a decent microphone and learn basic audio recording techniques. You need to minimize background noise, experiment with mic placement (shotgun for interviews, lavalier for on-the-go), and utilize editing software to clean up audio imperfections.

Microphone Placement:

For interviews, employ a lavalier microphone positioned close to the sound source, ensuring clear and direct audio capture. When dealing with distant audio, opt for a shotgun microphone to focus on the specific source while minimizing background noise. Experiment with microphone angles and distances to find the optimal setup for your specific recording environment.

Practical Setup: Attach the lavalier microphone discreetly to your subject's clothing, securing it near the

Wind Protection:

When shooting outdoors, guard against wind interference by using a windsock or furry muff on your microphone. This minimizes unwanted wind noise and ensures your audio remains crisp and clear.

Practical Setup: Slide the windsock over the microphone or attach a furry muff, making sure it covers the

Audio Recording Apps:

Enhance your audio recording capabilities by leveraging smartphone apps or dedicated audio recorders. These tools provide higher quality audio capture, allowing you to achieve professional sound quality even with minimal equipment.

Practical Setup: Download and install reputable audio recording apps on your smartphone, ensuring the

Editing Magic:

Learn essential audio editing techniques to refine your recordings in post-production. Master techniques like noise reduction, equalization, and level adjustments to clean up and enhance your audio quality.

Practical Setup: Import your recorded audio into a digital audio workstation (DAW) or editing soft

VARIETY IS THE SPICE OF LIFE: Break free from static tripod shots! Few things are more disengaging that seeing the same angle, over and over. Audience attention spans are constantly shrinking and its on us, my fellow docie-warriors, to make sure our visual are diverse and interesting enough to capture and retain their fleeting attention.

To do this, we will utilize camera movement to follow subjects, pan across landscapes, or create a sense of dynamism. Don't be afraid to even handhold shots for a more intimate feel.

Camera Movement:

Master the art of camera movement to bring dynamism to your shots. Follow your subject with smooth pans and tilts for a seamless and professional look. Add energy and engagement with well-timed zooms, or create a sense of urgency and immediacy with handheld shots.

Practical Setup: When using a tripod, ensure smooth pans and tilts by using a fluid head. Practice h

Static vs. Dynamic:

Balance static and dynamic shots to keep your viewers engaged. Utilize stable tripod shots for interviews, providing a solid and focused visual foundation. Break up static shots with handheld or moving sequences to inject energy and maintain audience interest.

Practical Setup: Set up your camera on a tripod for stable static shots during interviews. Introduce handl

___

Transitions and Sequences:

Plan your shots with an eye for transitions and sequences to create a cohesive narrative. Incorporate establishing shots, close-ups, and wide angles to guide your viewers seamlessly through the story.

Practical Setup: Develop a shot list or storyboard to visualize the flow of your documentary. Establish a c

___

Time-Lapses and Slow-Motion:

Experiment with time-lapse and slow-motion techniques to add a unique visual dimension to your footage. Use time-lapses to compress time, create a sense of drama, or showcase changing environments. Employ slow-motion for impactful moments, emphasizing details and providing a visually compelling texture to your scenes.

Practical Setup: Plan your time-lapse shots by selecting a compelling subject or scene that undergoes no

___

In the journey to master the intricate aspects of documentary filmmaking, remember that practice serves as your most valuable ally. The techniques discussed here, spanning camera movement, lighting mastery, and audio considerations, are not just theoretical concepts—they are tools in your creative arsenal. Experimentation is your playground; immerse yourself in diverse settings to witness firsthand how these techniques shape the visual impact of your shots.

As you delve into this hands-on learning process, you'll notice a transformation within yourself. The once unfamiliar concepts will become intuitive, ingrained in your filmmaking instincts. You'll develop a keen sense of when to employ smooth camera pans, how to harness the magic of natural light, and the art of crafting impactful audio. This intuitive mastery is the product of persistent exploration and application.

However, filmmaking is an ever-evolving journey, and challenges are an inherent part of the process. The next section will guide you in navigating the unexpected hurdles that may arise during a shoot. Embracing unexpected issues requires adaptability, problem-solving skills, and a resilient mindset. So, gear up for the unpredictable terrain that filmmaking sometimes presents, armed with the knowledge and practical skills you've cultivated thus far.

Embracing the Unexpected: When Plans Go South (and That's Okay):

In the unpredictable jungles of documentary filmmaking, encountering unexpected beasts and challenges is not a matter of "if" but "when." The ability to navigate these hurdles with the grace and resourcefulness of a season docie-warrior is an essential skill. Let's explore practical examples of such situations and tips on how to approach them:

TECHNICAL GREMLINS: Imagine you're in the midst of a crucial interview, and suddenly your camera decides to act up. Stay calm and troubleshoot! Before your shoot, familiarize yourself with basic equipment maintenance. Carry spare batteries, memory cards, and any necessary cables. Always have a backup option, like using your smartphone for filming if your main camera encounters technical difficulties. Remember, preparedness is your ally, and the ability to adapt on the spot can save the day.

Practical Example: Your primary camera battery unexpectedly dies during an interview. Quickly switch to a spare battery, and if that's not an option, smoothly transition to your smartphone for continuous recording.

LOGISTICAL DETOURS Filming on location comes with its own set of challenges, and logistics may not always go as planned. Be flexible! Adapt your schedule if permits are delayed, transportation falls through, or unforeseen events impact your filming location. Embrace the detours, as they may lead to unexpected and compelling footage that adds depth to your narrative.

Practical Example: Your planned outdoor shoot is interrupted by unexpected rain. Instead of canceling, adapt by finding an alternative indoor location or adjusting your schedule to capture the rain-soaked scenes, adding a unique element to your documentary.

ETHICAL TIGHTROPES In the pursuit of storytelling, ethical considerations are paramount. Remember that you're not just a filmmaker; you're a guest in people's lives. Prioritize informed consent, respect privacy, and navigate sensitive situations with empathy and awareness. Seek guidance when needed and always prioritize ethical storytelling practices.

Practical Example: You come across a personal moment during filming that could be emotionally sensitive for your subject. Pause the shoot and discuss the situation with your subject, ensuring they are comfortable proceeding. If needed, seek advice from a mentor or ethical guidelines to make informed decisions.

***

In essence, embracing the unexpected is not just about problem-solving but about transforming challenges into opportunities for richer storytelling. The ability to adapt, troubleshoot, and approach ethical dilemmas with sensitivity will not only define your resilience as a filmmaker but also contribute to the authenticity and depth of your documentary. Remember, the unexpected is often where the most profound stories unfold.

Exercise:

1. Storyboard a key scene: Sketch out the shots you envision for a specific scene, considering framing, composition, movement, and sound elements. This helps you plan your approach and anticipate potential challenges.
2. Challenge yourself with unscripted moments: Visit a local market, park, or event and practice capturing candid interactions, fleeting expressions, and unexpected moments of human connection. Don't be afraid to engage with people and let the story unfold organically.
3. Experiment with camera movement: Film a simple scene like someone making coffee or crossing a street. Try different types of camera movement (pans, tilts, zooms) and analyze how each technique affects the viewer's perception and emotional engagement.
4. Discuss your solo filming concerns: Share your worries and potential challenges with the community. Brainstorm creative solutions, learn from others' experiences, and build a network of support for your solo filmmaking

journey.

5. Watch and analyze: Immerse yourself in documentaries known for their captivating visuals and observational prowess. Analyze how the filmmakers utilize camera angles, lighting, and editing to tell their stories and evoke emotions. Learn from their successes and adapt their techniques to your own vision.

7

DAY 7

The Art of Interviewing

Most documentaries, at their core, are about the human experience. To get a clear understanding of people's stories you need to talk to them, people who know them or people who know and understand the subject you a tackling. You need to master the art of the interview.

Leave aside bland interviews and forced confessions and instead explore authentic voices, where every detail holds a story. Ditch the one-size-fits-all method and focus on crafting conversations that are meaningful by embracing the key element in every powerful documentary: relationships. To uncover someone's story, you need more than just a microphone. You need to be a trusted listener, someone who can draw out memories gently. We'll discuss building rapport, creating connections beyond the typical "interviewer-subject" setup.

But capturing stories is just the start. We'll also tackle the ethical challenges that come with using this powerful tool.

How do you balance honesty and sensitivity? How do you avoid manipulation and exploitation? We'll navigate these challenges together, providing you with a moral guide for your interview journey.

Lastly, get ready to turn those raw conversations into something magical. We'll cover active listening, asking the right questions (ones that resonate), and weaving these bits into a narrative that captivates audiences.

Starting an Interview: Creating Comfort and Connection

Embarking on an interview is like turning the key to a door that opens into the intimate spaces of someone's world. These initial moments serve as the threshold, shaping the atmosphere for the entire conversation and profoundly impacting the depth of insights that can be uncovered. The emotional value of your story, its hear and soul, hinge on your ability to make your interviewees comfortable and willing to shed their walls and bare their souls. To navigate this pivotal juncture with finesse, here are practical tips to establish a comfortable rapport and cultivate a meaningful connection right from the outset:

WARM WELCOME– SETTING THE TONE:

Begin with a warm welcome and a genuine expression of appreciation for their time. A warm welcome goes beyond mere courtesy; it establishes the foundation for a genuine exchange of ideas. It communicates that the interviewee is not merely a participant but a valued contributor whose insights are eagerly anticipated. This initial gesture sets the tone for openness, collaboration, and mutual respect—a foundation upon which a meaningful dialogue can flourish.

Expressing gratitude and excitement is an acknowledgment of the interviewee's time and contribution. For instance, "Thank you so much for joining us today. We're truly excited to hear your perspective on [insert topic here]," communicates genuine enthusiasm, fostering an environment where the interviewee feels their insights are anticipated with genuine interest. Here are a few tips on how to give your interviewees a warm welcome:

TONE OF VOICE:

Your voice is a powerful tool in conveying warmth. Ensure your tone is friendly, genuine, and resonates with enthusiasm. Avoid sounding scripted or detached; instead, let your tone reflect the authentic excitement you feel about engaging in this conversation.

BODY LANGUAGE:

Nonverbal cues often speak louder than words. Maintain eye contact to establish a connection and convey sincerity. A warm smile can go a long way in making the interviewee feel at ease. Pay attention to your posture; standing or sitting in an open and relaxed manner communicates approachability.

CHOICE OF WORDS:

The language you use sets the stage for the entire interaction. Choose words that express gratitude and eagerness. Use phrases like "We're thrilled to have you," or "Your insights are invaluable to us." Such language reinforces the idea that the interviewee's presence is not just welcomed but highly valued.

PERSONALIZATION:

Tailor your welcome to the specific context of the interviewee. Reference their work, achievements, or unique perspective. This personal touch not only demonstrates your preparation but also conveys that you see them as an individual with a distinct contribution to make.

INCLUSIVE ATMOSPHERE:

Make it clear that the interview is a collaborative effort. Use language that emphasizes shared exploration and mutual learning. Phrases like "Let's delve into this together," or "Your insights will guide our discussion," create a sense of partnership.

BE CURIOUS:

Beyond expressing excitement, convey curiosity about the interviewee's thoughts and experiences. A genuine interest in what they have to share makes them feel valued and encourages them to open up more freely.

ESTABLISHING COMMON GROUND

Find common ground or shared interests early in the conversation. This creates a sense of familiarity and helps bridge any initial gaps. It could be a shared experience, a common passion, or even a mutual acquaintance. Finding common ground is the bridge that spans the gap between interviewer and interviewee. It transforms the dynamic from an exchange of information to a shared exploration, creating an invitation to openness. This connection forms a subtle backdrop against which the interviewee can comfortably express their thoughts and experiences.

Referencing a shared interest isn't just a casual remark; it's an intentional effort to establish relatability. For instance, "I heard you're also a fan of [shared interest]. That's fantastic! I'd love to hear your thoughts on how it has influenced your perspective," not only highlights the commonality but extends an invitation for the interviewee to share their personal insights on a familiar subject. Heres how to naturally utilise shared interests without forcing a turn in the conversation that makes it feel shoe-horned in:

THOROUGH RESEARCH:

Prior to the interview, invest time in researching your interviewee. Explore their professional background, social media profiles, or any public statements they have made. Look for shared interests, affiliations, or experiences that can serve as potential points of connection.

BE SUBTLE:

Initiate the conversation by subtly introducing a shared interest. This could be a hobby, a professional achievement, or a common acquaintance. For example, "I came across your work in [specific area], and I'm fascinated by your approach. I noticed we both share an interest in [shared interest]."

ENTHUSIASM IS THE KEY:

When mentioning the shared interest, express genuine enthusiasm. Use language that conveys your appreciation for that shared aspect. This authenticity helps in creating a sense of sincerity and interest, making the connection more meaningful.

FLEXIBLE ADAPTATION:

Be flexible in adapting your approach based on the interviewee's responses. If they seem particularly passionate about a specific shared interest, allow the conversation to naturally evolve in that direction. This flexibility ensures that the common ground serves as a dynamic foundation rather than a rigid script.

HIGHLIGHT SHARED EXPERIENCES:

Beyond interests, acknowledge shared experiences if applicable. This could be attending the same event, facing similar challenges, or having mutual connections. Such shared experiences deepen the sense of relatability.

EXPLORE SHARED VALUES:

Identify and reflect shared values during the conversation. This could be a commitment to a certain cause, a similar approach to problem-solving, or a shared ethos. Reflecting these shared values reinforces the sense of connection.

CLARIFY THE PROCESS

Uncertainty can cast a shadow over the interviewee's ability to express themselves freely. By articulating the interview process clearly, you provide a framework that acts as a steady anchor, allowing the interviewee to navigate the conversation with confidence. This transparency transforms the interview from an unknown venture into a collaborative and predictable experience.

Explicitly stating what topics will be covered and encouraging the interviewee to share comfortably is more than a courtesy; it's an invitation for them to actively participate in shaping the conversation. For example, "During our conversation today, we'll cover [topics]. Feel free to share as much or as little as you're comfortable with, and we can adjust as needed," communicates openness, flexibility, and a genuine willingness to adapt to the interviewee's comfort level.

INTRODUCE THE INTERVIEW STRUCTURE:

At the beginning of the interview, provide a brief overview of the structure. Mention the key topics that will be covered, ensuring that the interviewee has a clear understanding of the conversation's direction.

CLARIFY DURATION:

Clearly communicate the expected duration of the interview. Whether it's a concise discussion or a more in-depth conversation, informing the interviewee of the time commitment helps manage expectations and allows them to mentally prepare.

EXPRESS THE SPIRIT OF COLLABORATION:

Express that the conversation is a collaborative effort, emphasizing that the interviewee's input is highly valued. This empowers the interviewee to steer the conversation based on their comfort level.

OPENLY ACKNOWLEDGE ADAPTABILITY:

Acknowledge that the interview format is adaptable. Assure the interviewee that the discussion is not bound by a rigid script, and adjustments can be made based on their preferences or any unexpected directions the conversation may take.

ADDRESS SENSITIVE TOPICS:

If there are potential sensitive topics to be discussed, address them upfront. Mention your awareness of these topics and express a commitment to handling them with care. This proactive approach builds trust and allows the interviewee to prepare emotionally.

MAKE IT A CONVERSATION:

Before the interview begins, open the floor for any questions or clarifications the interviewee may have about the process. This demonstrates a commitment to transparency and ensures that they feel informed and empowered throughout the interview.

ICEBREAKER QUESTIONS- LIGHTENING THE ATMOSPHERE

Kick off with light and non-intrusive icebreaker questions. These can be casual inquiries that allow your interviewee to share personal anecdotes or preferences, helping them ease into the conversation.The opening moments can set the tone for the entire conversation, and icebreaker questions play a crucial role in breaking down initial barriers.

The choice of the icebreaker question is not arbitrary; it's a strategic move to engage the interviewee in a way that is enjoyable and relatable. For example, "Before we dive into the main discussion, let's start with something fun. What's a favorite hobby or interest of yours outside of [main topic]?" not only invites the interviewee to share but also sets a positive and relaxed tone for the upcoming dialogue.

TAILOR QUESTIONS TO PERSONAL INTERESTS:

Customize your icebreaker questions to align with the interviewee's personality and known interests. This demonstrates that you've done your homework and are genuinely interested in them as an individual.

CHOOSE NON-INTRUSIVE TOPICS:

Opt for topics that are light-hearted and non-intrusive. Avoid diving into personal or sensitive areas too soon. Consider asking about hobbies, interests, or preferences that are likely to evoke positive and enjoyable responses.

SUBTLY RELATE ICEBREAKERS TO THE MAIN TOPIC:

Whenever possible, subtly connect the icebreaker questions to the main topics of the interview. This helps in transitioning smoothly from the light-hearted opening to the more substantive aspects of the conversation.

SHARE YOUR OWN RESPONSES:

To foster a sense of reciprocity, consider sharing your own response to the icebreaker questions. This adds a personal touch to the interaction and creates a more conversational atmosphere. Respond actively to the interviewee's answers. Express genuine interest, ask follow-up questions, or share your own thoughts related to their response. This engagement helps in building a connection from the outset.

ENCOURAGE ANECDOTES:

Structure your icebreaker questions to encourage the interviewee to share stories. This not only adds depth to the conversation but also establishes a narrative flow from the very beginning.

MAINTAIN A POSITIVE TONE:

Ensure that the overall tone of the icebreaker is positive and uplifting. Aim to create an atmosphere where the interviewee feels comfortable and even excited to share more about themselves.

BE MINDFUL OF CULTURAL SENSITIVITIES:

Consider the cultural background of the interviewee when crafting icebreaker questions. Be mindful of any cultural sensitivities to ensure that the chosen topics are inclusive and respectful.

As a budding docie-warrior, it's essential to recognize that these initial moments are not just a formality but a gateway to a genuine exchange of ideas. By extending a warm welcome, finding common ground, clarifying the process, and incorporating icebreaker questions, you set the stage for a collaborative and comfortable dialogue.

As you embark on your documentarian journey, remember that

each interaction is an opportunity to connect with the unique perspectives of your subjects. The warmth you infuse into these moments is not just a nicety but a catalyst for authentic storytelling. A welcoming environment communicates that you value not only the information your subjects provide but also their individuality and experiences.

So, as you approach your next interview, let the welcome be more than words; let it be a gesture that echoes throughout the conversation. Through these intentional and thoughtful practices, you pave the way for a storytelling experience that is not only informative but also engaging, relatable, and deeply human.

In the next section, we'll delve into the intricacies of the interview itself, exploring how to navigate various aspects such as active listening, asking powerful questions, and addressing ethical considerations.

Unleashing the Power of Conversation:

BEYOND THE SURFACE:

To truly capture the essence of your subject's story, you need to go beyond the basic facts and figures. Ask open-ended questions that encourage reflection and the sharing of personal anecdotes. For instance, instead of asking, "What was your experience like?" you might inquire, "Can you walk me through a specific moment that left a lasting impact on you?"

This invites your interviewee to delve into their memories, offering more nuanced and revealing insights.

Practical Example: If you're documenting someone's journey overcoming adversity, ask them to describe a particular challenge they faced and how it shaped their perspective.

Formulate questions that prompt storytelling rather than simple yes or no answers. Encourage interviewees to share their thoughts, feelings, and personal experiences.

FOLLOW THE EMOTIONAL THREAD:

Authenticity often lies in unexpected tangents and emotional shifts. Don't be afraid to follow these threads during your interview. If your subject expresses a sudden emotion or takes an unexpected turn in the conversation, explore it further. These moments can lead to powerful and revealing insights that add depth to your documentary.

Practical Example: If your interviewee unexpectedly becomes emotional when discussing a specific event, gently probe further by asking, "Can you tell me more about what you're feeling in this moment?"

Stay flexible in your questioning, allowing the conversation to evolve naturally. Be attuned to emotional cues, and be ready to explore areas that may not have been initially planned.

SILENCE IS YOUR ALLY

Resist the urge to fill every pause in the conversation. The true docie-warrior knows that ilence provides a valuable space for your interviewee to gather their thoughts and express emotions. When you allow these moments of quiet, you might be surprised at the depth and authenticity that can emerge.

Practical Example: After asking a thought-provoking question, give your interviewee a few moments of silence before prompting them to share their response. This can encourage more considered and genuine answers.

Embrace pauses as opportunities for reflection. Avoid interrupting or rushing to the next question. Let the silence create a comfortable environment for open and honest communication.

PRACTICE ACTIVE LISTENING:

Active listening goes beyond hearing words. Pay close attention to nonverbal cues such as micro-expressions, changes in vocal tone, and body language. These subtle indicators often reveal unspoken emotions and provide valuable insights into your subject's thoughts and experiences.

Practical Example: If your interviewee's tone changes when discussing a certain topic, explore that shift by asking, "I noticed a change in your voice. Can you elaborate on what you're feeling right now?"

Train yourself to observe nonverbal cues during interviews. Develop a keen awareness of the emotional nuances conveyed through body language and tone. This heightened sensitivity can lead to more profound storytelling.

As we conclude our exploration of techniques to go beyond the surface and truly capture the essence of your subjects' stories, it's crucial to recognize the transformative power of thoughtful interviewing. By asking open-ended questions, following emotional threads, embracing silence, and practicing active listening, you embark on a journey of discovery that transcends mere information-gathering.

Delving into the practical applications of these principles, such as formulating questions that prompt storytelling and encouraging interviewees to share their thoughts and feelings, you set the stage for narratives that resonate on a profound level. Your role as a docie-warrior extends beyond traditional interviewing; it becomes a dynamic dance of curiosity, empathy, and receptiveness.

REVISION

We have already explored camera techniques in previous chapters, but its vital for your warrior's journey to rehash elements of your training and contextualize them with each increment in your knowledge of the way of the docie-warrior. Lets reconsider the following concepts:

CAPTURING THE ESSENCE ON CAMERA:

SHOW DON'T TELL: Utilize visuals beyond the talking head. Capture reactions, environmental details, and symbolic elements that visually enrich the interview's context and emotional impact.

VARIETY IS THE SPICE OF LIFE: Break up static shots with subtle camera movements, zooms, and close-ups that add dynamism and keep viewers engaged. Consider utilizing B-roll footage (supplementary visuals) to further illustrate the interviewee's story.

LIGHT FOR MOOD: Create an atmosphere that complements the

interview's tone. Warm lighting for intimate conversations, dramatic shadows for intense moments, and natural light for authenticity - use light as a storytelling tool.

UTILIZE IMMERSIVE SOUND DESIGN: Pay attention to audio quality. Minimize background noise, utilize proper mic placement, and explore creative sound effects or music to enhance the emotional depth of your interview.

ETHICAL CONSIDERATIONS:

INFORMED CONSENT IS KEY: Clearly explain the purpose of your project, how their footage will be used, and ensure they understand their right to stop filming or edit their responses. Consider written consent forms for added clarity.

VULNERABILITY WITH RESPECT: Recognize the vulnerability your interviewees entrust you with. Handle sensitive topics with discretion, avoid sensationalism, and prioritize their well-being above your narrative goals.

BALANCING PERSPECTIVES: Strive for objectivity. Present different viewpoints, avoid manipulation, and ensure your interviewee's voice is represented authentically. Seek diverse perspectives to enrich your storytelling.

CONFIDENTIALITY MATTERS: Maintaining confidentiality is paramount. Always exercise caution when considering the disclosure of sensitive information, and discuss confidentiality agreements if needed. If your interviewee wishes to remain anonymous, take appropriate measures such as having them face away from the camera, avoiding lighting that reveals recognizable features, and, during editing, altering their voice and blurring their face to protect their identity.

****

As we conclude this day, remember that the journey of mastering the art of interviewing mirrors the path of a warrior continuously refining their skills. The quest for proficiency is an ongoing expedition, one marked by the pursuit of ethical awareness and the cultivation of genuine human connections.

Armed with the knowledge gained here, envision yourself as a docie-warrior, weaving the threads of empathy and skill into the fabric of each interview. Much like the African warrior who hones their craft through experience, you too will refine your techniques, ensuring each conversation becomes a cinematic moment that resonates deeply.

This journey extends beyond mere technique; it's about capturing the essence of your subject's story. As you go forth, remember that your role is not just that of an interviewer but a storyteller, breathing life into moments that linger in the minds of your audience.

In the realm of solo documentaries, the power of your conversations lies not just in information but in the emotional impact they carry. Channel the spirit of the docie-warrior, armed not with weapons but with the finesse of words and the compassion of understanding.

Exercise:

1. Develop a detailed interview guide: Research your subject, identify key themes, and craft open-ended questions that delve into their experiences and emotions. Include follow-up prompts to explore unexpected turns in the conversation.

2. Practice active listening in everyday interactions: Engage actively in conversations, truly listen without judgment, and observe nonverbal cues. Notice how active listening deepens your understanding and fosters genuine connection.

3. Set up a mock interview environment: Choose a willing participant, experiment with different camera angles, lighting setups, and sound recording techniques. Analyze the impact of each choice on the interview's visual and emotional tone.

4. Discuss ethical dilemmas with the community: Share potential challenges, exchange strategies for navigating sensitive topics, and learn from each other's experiences to ensure ethical storytelling practices throughout your journey.

5. Analyze interview techniques in impactful documentaries: Watch documentaries known for their powerful conversations and dissect how the filmmakers utilize framing, lighting, sound design, and editing to elevate the interview's emotional impact and draw viewers into the story.

8

DAY 8

B-Roll Brilliance - Mastering the Narrative Power of Visuals

Welcome back Docie-warrior! Today, we're diving into a crucial aspect of crafting compelling documentaries – B-roll footage. It's not just filler; it's the secret weapon that turns your documentary into a visual story, and in this chapter, we're breaking down the essentials of B-roll, demystifying advanced techniques, tackling logistics, and showing you how to wield it like a true Docie-warrior.

B-roll isn't the star, but it's the sidekick that makes your lead shine. It's the visual poetry that adds layers to your storytelling. Think of it like a tool in your kit – enhancing your skills and making your documentary visually captivating.

Essential B-Roll Techniques for Solo Success:

In the expansive world of documentary filmmaking, B-roll transcends its role as supplementary footage; it stands as a key element in unlocking a visual narrative that extends far beyond the limitations of interviews alone. Let's delve deeper into the essence of B-roll, uncovering how it breathes life into your story by capturing details that interviews cannot fully convey.

BEYOND TALKING HEADS:

B-roll breathes life into your story by showcasing details your interviews can't fully capture. Capture establishing shots, evocative landscapes, and symbolic elements that enrich your narrative's context and texture.

1. *Establishing Shots:*

Establishing shots serve as the cinematic overture to your documentary, setting the stage and immersing your audience in the visual landscape of your narrative. These wide-angle glimpses are not just about locations; they encapsulate the essence of your documentary's theme. For example, if your documentary explores the pulse of a city, an establishing shot capturing its skyline or bustling streets becomes the visual prelude, providing context before plunging into the interviews.

Practical Insight: To maximize the impact of establishing shots, consider factors such as time of day, weather, and framing. A well-crafted establishing shot not only introduces your audience to the setting but also establishes the mood and tone of your documentary.

2. *Evocative Landscapes:*

B-roll goes beyond the mundane, allowing you to showcase landscapes that evoke emotions and deepen your storytelling. We have already established the power of an establishing shot, but now consider applying that same power to enhancing an emotional beat or to give your audience a breath after a massive revelation a=or thought provoking moment. Whether it's the serenity of a forest, the vastness of a desert, or the majesty of a mountain range, evocative landscapes provide a sensory experience that complements the narrative arc of your documentary.

Practical Insight: Choose landscapes that resonate with the emotional beats of your story. If your documentary explores resilience, consider capturing natural landscapes that symbolize strength and endurance, creating a visual backdrop that resonates with the overarching theme.

3. *Symbolic Elements:*

In the realm of B-roll, symbolic elements act as visual metaphors enrich the texture of your story. Each carefully chosen symbol becomes a potent tool to convey nuanced messages. For instance, a weathered book might represent history, a flickering candle- hope, or a bustling marketplace community – each adding layers of meaning that enhance the narrative depth.

Practical Insight: Identify key themes in your documentary and brainstorm symbolic elements that align with those themes. Symbolism in B-roll can be subtle yet powerful, offering viewers an additional layer of interpretation that enriches their engagement with your narrative. For example, instead of simply having a character discuss innocence, show symbolic B-roll of children's art painted on walls or paper to convey the idea of innocence.

4. *Enhancing Emotional Resonance:*
One of the most potent aspects of B-roll is its ability to evoke emotions without uttering a word. The selection of visuals – whether it's the warmth of a sunrise, the hustle of a busy market, or the tranquility of a deserted landscape – amplifies the emotional resonance of your documentary.

Practical Insight: Align your B-roll with the emotional tone you want to convey. If your narrative explores moments of introspection, incorporate footage of quiet, contemplative spaces. Experiment with different visuals to discern the emotional impact they bring, ensuring they harmonize with the overall tone of your documentary.

VISUAL STORYTELLING WITHOUT WORDS:
In the intricate realm of documentary filmmaking, the art of visual storytelling without words takes center stage. This section unravels the significance of letting your visuals speak volumes, particularly through the potent medium of B-roll. Powerful B-roll has the capacity to convey emotions, ideas, and themes without solely relying on narration, introducing a layer of depth and complexity to your storytelling.

1. *Conveying Emotions:*
Silent narratives through B-roll offer a compelling means to convey emotions that words may struggle to articulate. Whether it's the joy of a reunion, the solitude of a contemplative moment, or the tension of a pivotal event, carefully chosen visuals become the brushstrokes that paint an emotional canvas for your audience.

Practical Insight: Experiment with capturing a range of emotions through B-roll. Consider the pacing, framing, and composition of each shot to ensure that the emotional nuances are conveyed effectively. For instance, a slow pan across a crowded room can evoke a sense of isolation or longing, adding a poignant emotional layer to your documentary.

Imagine a poignant reunion scene in a documentary about family dynamics. Instead of relying solely on interviews and verbal expressions, the use of B-roll can be transformative. The slow-motion embrace, tears welling up, and shared smiles during the reunion can convey a spectrum of emotions without a single spoken word. The visuals become a silent narrative that speaks directly to the audience's hearts, evoking empathy and connection.

2. *Conveying Ideas:*

B-roll transcends the limitations of verbal expression, becoming a visual language that communicates complex ideas seamlessly. Whether it's illustrating historical events, showcasing scientific processes, or depicting societal dynamics, visuals can simplify intricate concepts, making them accessible and engaging for your audience.

Practical Insight: When tasked with conveying abstract ideas, break them down into visual components. Create a sequence of B-roll shots that progressively build upon each other, gradually forming a coherent representation of the idea. This method allows your audience to grasp complex concepts without the need for extensive verbal explanation.

Consider a documentary delving into the intricacies of a scientific breakthrough. Instead of drowning the audience in technical jargon through narration, B-roll becomes the visual translator. Shots of researchers in a lab, intricate experiments unfolding, and the eureka moment captured on scientists' faces convey the essence of the breakthrough. Viewers grasp complex ideas without words, allowing the visual narrative to engage and educate simultaneously.

3. *Conveying Themes:*

Themes, the underlying threads that weave through your documentary, can be powerfully communicated through B-roll. Instead of explicitly stating a theme through narration, let the visuals subtly introduce and reinforce these overarching concepts. This not only engages your audience on a visual level but also encourages them to interpret and connect with the themes independently.

Practical Insight: Identify key themes in your documentary and brainstorm corresponding visual motifs. For instance, if your documentary explores the theme of resilience, integrate B-roll footage showcasing elements of endurance, growth, and overcoming challenges. Allow these visuals to organically reinforce the thematic fabric of your storytelling.

In a documentary exploring societal changes, the theme of unity can be subtly conveyed through B-roll. Instead of explicitly stating the theme, visuals can depict diverse individuals coming together in shared spaces, collaborative efforts, and moments of collective celebration. These visuals act as silent motifs, allowing the audience to connect with the theme organically and draw their interpretations from the visual tapestry.

4. *Adding Depth and Complexity:*

B-roll introduces a layer of depth and complexity to your

storytelling by allowing for nuanced interpretations. While narration provides explicit information, visuals invite viewers to infer and immerse themselves in the narrative, creating a more interactive and engaging viewing experience.

Practical Insight: When crafting B-roll sequences, consider the layers of meaning each shot contributes. Avoid overly explicit visuals, encouraging your audience to actively participate in deciphering the narrative. This collaborative interpretation adds richness to your documentary, sparking curiosity and fostering a deeper connection with your viewers.

Consider a documentary on environmental conservation, where the theme of interconnectedness is central. Instead of verbalizing the concept, B-roll footage can showcase the intricate ecosystems at play – the symbiotic relationships between flora and fauna, the delicate balance of nature. The shots could trace the food chain and relate plants and creatures by how they depend on each other for survival. Each shot adds layers of meaning, inviting viewers to explore the depth and complexity of the subject matter on their own terms.

MASTERING COMPOSITION AND FRAMING:

There is a saying among the Shona tribes of Zimbabwe "Dzokororo ine simba", which roughly translates to " There is power in repetition". With those wise words in mind, lets delve once more into the intricacies of composition, only this time, from a b-roll perspective.

When it comes to acquiring stellar B-roll for your solo documentary, delving into the intricacies of composition and framing is paramount. It goes beyond the basics and involves utilizing principles like the rule of thirds, leading lines, and unexpected angles. These elements become the foundation for visually compelling shots that not only capture attention but immerse viewers in the narrative. Let's explore each facet in the context of enhancing your B-roll and provide practical insights to guide your journey toward mastery.

1. *Rule of Thirds:*

In the realm of B-roll, employing the rule of thirds can transform your footage into visually captivating sequences. Instead of centering your subject, position them along the grid lines or intersections. This technique brings balance and intrigue to your shots, making them more dynamic and engaging.

Practical Insight: Imagine capturing B-roll of a bustling market scene for a documentary on local economies. Instead of placing the market center-frame, position it along the grid lines, allowing the viewers to absorb the vibrancy of the surroundings while maintaining a balanced composition. Or, imagine showcasing a craftsman at work. Place the hands and tools along the intersections, creating a visually engaging composition.

2. *Leading Lines:*

Leading lines guide the viewer's gaze through your B-roll, creating a visual narrative within the sequence. Whether it's a winding road or the flow of a river, leverage leading lines to draw attention to key elements in your documentary. These lines act as visual cues, enhancing the storytelling aspect of your B-roll.

Practical Insight: Suppose your solo documentary explores the concept of journey and exploration. Capture B-roll of a subject walking along a path with prominent leading lines. This not only provides a visual narrative of movement but also subtly reinforces the thematic elements of your documentary.

To nail the idea home, here is another example; film B-roll of a subject traversing through a dynamic environment, such as a cityscape. Utilize the lines formed by buildings, streets, or natural elements to guide the viewer's gaze. This not only adds visual interest but also subtly underscores the subject's journey.

3. *Unexpected Angles:*

To infuse dynamism into your B-roll, experiment with unexpected angles that offer fresh perspectives. Break away from conventional shots and explore unique viewpoints. Whether it's a low angle to emphasize power or a high angle for a bird's-eye view, these unexpected angles add depth and interest to your footage.

Practical Insight: If your documentary focuses on innovation and creativity, consider shooting B-roll from a low angle, showcasing hands at work with tools and materials. This unexpected perspective not only adds visual interest but emphasizes the uniqueness and creativity of the subject matter. As another example, suppose your solo documentary delves into the beauty of nature. Experiment with an unexpected angle, perhaps a close-up shot of a flower or a tree branch, captured from a low angle. This not only adds a unique perspective but also brings viewers closer to the intricate details of the natural world.

SHOTS TO SET THE MOOD:

Setting the right mood and tone is an art that B-roll mastery can elevate. It involves utilizing B-roll to create specific atmospheres that resonate with your narrative by making appropriate shot choices for appropriate instances. Whether it's panoramic shots for majestic landscapes, intimate close-ups for personal moments, or dynamic movements for action sequences, each visual choice contributes to setting the emotional tone of your scenes.

1. *Panoramic Shots for Majestic Landscapes:*

For capturing the grandeur of vast landscapes or significant settings in your documentary, employ panoramic shots. These shots provide a sweeping view, allowing your audience to absorb the majesty of the environment and setting the stage for impactful storytelling.

How to Do It:

- Use a tripod to ensure stability and avoid shaky footage.
- Choose a wide-angle lens (around 24mm to 35mm) for capturing expansive views. you can go even wider (12mm), but this depends on how you like your visuals to come across.
- Set your camera to a low ISO to maintain image quality, especially in well-lit outdoor settings.
- Begin with a horizontal sweep, keeping the movement smooth and controlled.
- Experiment with different angles to find the most captivating perspective.
- Optionally, consider using slow-motion (High frame rate footage, like 60-120fps, slowed down in the edit) for added cinematic effect.

Practical Insight: In a documentary exploring the wonders of nature, use panoramic B-roll to showcase expansive landscapes like mountain ranges, seascapes, or sprawling forests. This not only establishes the geographical context but also sets a tone of awe and appreciation.

2. Close-Ups for Intimate Moments:

To convey the intimacy of personal narratives or emotional moments, leverage close-up shots in your B-roll. These shots focus on the subtle details, expressions, and interactions that intensify the emotional connection between the audience and the subject.

How to Do It:

- Choose a lens with a wide aperture (e.g., 50mm at f/1.8) for a shallow depth of field.
- Physically get close to the subject to capture intimate details and expressions.
- Focus on facial expressions, gestures, or objects that carry emotional significance.
- Ensure adequate lighting to highlight details without harsh shadows.
- Experiment with various angles to convey the desired emotion.

Practical Insight: Suppose your solo documentary delves into personal stories of overcoming adversity. Use close-up B-roll to capture facial expressions, gestures, or objects that carry emotional significance, creating an intimate connection between the audience and the subject.

3. *Dynamic Movements for Action Sequences:*

In sequences requiring a sense of action, energy, or movement, incorporate dynamic shots into your B-roll. These shots can include tracking movements, dynamic pans, or quick cuts, creating a visual rhythm that aligns with the pace and energy of the scene.

How to Do It:

- Use a stabilizer or gimbal to ensure smooth and stable tracking shots.
- Incorporate dynamic camera movements like pans, tilts, or zooms to add energy to the footage.
- Experiment with quick cuts between different activities to create a visual rhythm.
- Adjust camera settings for the desired mood; for dynamic shots, consider a faster shutter speed.
- Optionally, use slow-motion for impactful action sequences.

Practical Insight: If your documentary involves action-oriented themes, such as sports or community events, integrate dynamic B-roll movements. Capture the fast-paced action, intricate details, and the overall vibrancy of the scene to set a tone of excitement and energy.

Examples:

1. **Panoramic Shots:** Imagine crafting a documentary on cultural heritage, focusing on historical monuments. Utilize panoramic B-roll shots to reveal the grandeur of architec-

tural marvels, creating a sense of awe and emphasizing the cultural significance of the subject.

2. **Close-Ups:** In a documentary centered around personal achievements, employ close-up B-roll during key moments of triumph or reflection. Capture the nuances of facial expressions, the clenching of fists, or the shedding of tears to convey the emotional depth of the individual's journey.

3. **Dynamic Movements:** Suppose your solo documentary explores the vitality of a bustling urban community. Utilize dynamic B-roll movements, such as tracking shots through crowded streets or quick cuts between various activities, to encapsulate the energetic and vibrant atmosphere of the city.

BRIDGING THE GAPS:

B-roll helps smooth transitions between interviews, locations, or time periods. This technique ensures a continuous and engaging narrative flow, connecting seemingly disparate elements into a cohesive visual story.

1. *Creative Cuts:*

Creative cuts in B-roll involve strategic editing to transition between scenes or subjects seamlessly. This technique ensures that the viewer experiences a fluid and connected narrative, avoiding abrupt shifts. Whether it's a match cut, where elements in successive shots complement each other, or a jump cut for intentional stylistic choices, creative cuts maintain the flow of your documentary.

How to Do It:

- Identify key moments or visual elements that serve as transition points.
- Use creative cuts to smoothly transition from one scene to another.
- Experiment with matching action or visual motifs for a cohesive effect.
- Ensure that the pacing aligns with the overall rhythm of your documentary.

Practical Insight: Suppose your solo documentary delves into the contrast between urban and rural life. Utilize creative cuts to smoothly transition between footage of a bustling city street and a tranquil countryside scene. This technique not only bridges the gap but also accentuates the thematic elements of your documentary. Alternatively use a creative cut from a historical photograph discussed in the interview to a matching contemporary shot of the location. This cut visually bridges the gap between the past and present seamlessly.

2. *Dissolves:*

Dissolves offer a subtle yet effective way to transition between different B-roll shots. By gradually blending one image into another, dissolves create a sense of continuity and harmony. This technique is particularly useful when transitioning between interviews or capturing changes in mood or tone within your narrative.

How to Do It:

- Employ dissolves to create a gradual transition between two shots.
- Select shots that share a thematic or visual connection for a smoother dissolve.
- Adjust the dissolve duration based on the desired mood and narrative pace.
- Use dissolves to evoke a sense of continuity, especially when transitioning across different time periods.

Practical Insight: In a documentary exploring the passage of time or a transformative journey, use dissolves to transition between relevant B-roll shots. For example, dissolve from a sunrise to a bustling city, symbolizing a new beginning or a change in narrative direction. You could also introduce a dissolve between the closing frame of an interview and the opening frame of another event. This subtle transition helps maintain viewer engagement while signaling a shift in time.

3. *Montages:*

B-roll montages involve combining a series of shots to condense time, convey emotion, or highlight multiple aspects of your narrative. Montages are powerful tools for maintaining engagement and conveying information efficiently. Whether showcasing a character's development or illustrating a complex process, montages offer a dynamic way to bridge gaps in your documentary.

How to Do It:

- Curate a series of related B-roll shots to form a thematic montage.

- Ensure the montage serves a storytelling purpose, bridging gaps in information.
- Use montages to convey the passage of time, changes in mood, or shifts in focus.
- Pay attention to the rhythm and progression within the montage for maximum impact.

Practical Insight: If your solo documentary covers a historical event or a significant transformation, create a B-roll montage to capture key moments or milestones. This not only serves as an engaging visual sequence but also aids in transitioning between different phases of your narrative.

FOr a documentary that covers a project, you could create a montage incorporating B-roll clips showing different stages of the project – from planning meetings to groundbreaking ceremonies. This montage efficiently communicates progress over time, keeping the audience connected to the project's narrative.

Conquering Solo B-Roll Challenges:

- **Planning and Resourcefulness:** Storyboard your B-roll needs beforehand and utilize available resources. Public spaces, libraries, and even your own backyard can offer stunning visuals with a bit of creativity.

- **Time Management:** Prioritize capturing essential B-roll while filming interviews. Consider shooting additional footage during location visits or dedicating specific days to capturing visuals.
- **Technical Limitations:** Work with what you have! Learn to utilize your camera's capabilities, experiment with DIY lighting solutions, and consider free or affordable editing software that offers basic color grading tools.
- **Keeping it Relevant:** Avoid unnecessary filler footage. Every shot should contribute to your narrative or evoke a specific emotion. Prioritize quality over quantity and ensure your B-roll directly serves your story.

Advanced B-Roll Techniques for Storytelling Depth:

Now lets explore some extra tips (some of which were casually mentioned earlier but not expanded on) that will take your now prestine B-roll to even higher levels.

TIME LAPSES AND SLOW MOTION:

Incorporating time-lapses and slow-motion sequences into your B-roll arsenal adds a dynamic layer to your solo documentary, capturing the nuanced essence of the passing moments. Here's a comprehensive guide, including practical advice, insights, and examples for effectively utilizing these techniques:

TIME LAPSE:

- *Camera and Lens:* Use a camera with manual exposure

control and a sturdy tripod. A wide-angle lens is ideal for capturing expansive scenes. Consider an intervalometer for precise control.

- *Settings*: Opt for a lower ISO to minimize noise, choose a small aperture for depth of field, and adjust the shutter speed based on the scene's brightness. Experiment with different intervals to suit the pace of the event.

Practical Insight:

Capture the sunrise over a city skyline to emphasize the transformation from darkness to light. A well-executed time-lapse can condense a visually stunning event into a brief and impactful sequence, setting the tone for your narrative.

SLOW MOTION:

- *Camera and Lens*: Choose a camera with high-frame-rate capabilities. A lens with a wide aperture enables more light, crucial for maintaining image quality in slow-motion.
- *Settings*: Set a high frame rate (e.g., 120 fps or more) for smooth slow-motion footage. Adjust the shutter speed to maintain the desired level of motion blur. (Ideally, SHutter speed should be twice the frame rate e.g. 120 fps= 1/240, 60fps=1/120 and 25fps=1/50

Practical Insight:

Capture the delicate flutter of a butterfly's wings or the expressive details of a craftsman's hands at work. Slow-motion can amplify subtle movements, allowing viewers to appreciate the intricate beauty or skill within your narrative.

MACRO CLOSE UPS:

Macro close-ups offer an intimate view of your subject, revealing hidden details that add richness to your narrative. Here's how to effectively incorporate macro close-ups into your B-roll:

- *Camera and Lens*: Use a macro lens for detailed close-ups. Ensure stability with a tripod, especially in low light conditions.
- *Settings*: Choose a wide aperture (e.g., f/2.8) for a shallow depth of field, isolating the subject from the background. Adjust ISO and shutter speed based on lighting conditions.

Practical Insight:

Zoom in on raindrops clinging to a leaf, capturing the texture and reflections. Macro close-ups can convey the tangible details of nature, human expression, or intricate objects, fostering a deeper connection with your audience.

DRONE FOOTAGE:

Drone footage provides a majestic perspective, offering sweeping panoramas and unique angles that add scale and awe to your solo documentary. Here's a guide to effectively incorporate drone shots:

- *Regulations:* Familiarize yourself with local regulations and obtain necessary permits before flying a drone.
- *Planning:* Plan shots carefully, considering the trajectory, altitude, and framing for a cinematic impact. If you can't fly a drone (or don't own one), consider partnering with a drone pilot.

Practical Insight:

Showcase the vastness of a natural landscape or the intricate details of an urban environment. Drone footage can capture dynamic scenes, providing a breathtaking visual context that complements your narrative.

RHYTHM AND PACING

Mastering rhythm and pacing in your B-roll is akin to conducting a visual symphony, orchestrating different elements to create a harmonious narrative flow. Here's a comprehensive guide with practical advice, insights, and examples for effectively integrating rhythm and pacing into your solo documentary:

RHYTHM:

- *Diversify Shot Lengths:* Mix short, dynamic shots with longer, contemplative ones. This diversity creates a visual cadence, preventing monotony.

- *Experiment with Camera Movements*: Introduce varied camera movements, such as pans, tilts, or tracking shots, to infuse energy and rhythm into your sequences.
- *Use Editing Cuts Deliberately*: Employ cuts strategically to match the rhythm of the scene. Quick cuts can convey urgency, while slower transitions evoke reflection.
- *Varying Shot Durations:* Adjust the duration of each shot to control the pacing. Quick succession of shots intensifies the pace, while lingering on a frame slows it down.
- *Consider the Emotional Tone*: Match the pacing to the emotional tone of your narrative. Reflective moments may benefit from a slower pace, while action sequences demand a brisk rhythm.
- *Storyboard for Pacing*: Plan the pacing during pre-production by storyboarding your B-roll sequences. This visual road map helps maintain a cohesive pace.

Practical Insight:

In a documentary exploring the daily routine of a bustling market, employ short, lively shots of transactions, interspersed with longer, observational shots of the market's atmosphere. This rhythm mirrors the dynamic nature of the setting. Alternatively, consider a documentary exploring the life of an artist, a slow-paced B-roll sequence showcasing the artist immersed in their work can create a contemplative and immersive experience.

SOUND DESIGN AND MUSIC:

The synergy between visuals and sound is a powerful aspect

of documentary filmmaking. Incorporating sound design and music into your B-roll enhances emotional impact and integrates the visuals seamlessly into the overall soundscape. Here's a guide on how to effectively utilize sound:

SOUND DESIGN:

- *Capture Ambient Sounds:* Record ambient sounds during B-roll shooting. These natural sounds immerse viewers in the environment and add authenticity.
- *Add Subtle Sound Effects*: Incorporate subtle sound effects to emphasize specific actions or elements within the B-roll. Ensure they enhance rather than distract from the visuals.

Practical Insight:

In a documentary portraying a rainy day, include the gentle patter of raindrops or distant thunder as part of your B-roll sound design. These elements contribute to the atmospheric storytelling.

MUSIC:

- *Choose Music Thoughtfully*: Select music that complements the mood and theme of your documentary. Ensure it doesn't overpower the visuals but enhances the emotional resonance.
- *Consider Music Transitions*: Plan transitions between different B-roll sequences with music in mind. Smooth transitions maintain a cohesive soundscape.

Practical Insight:

If your documentary explores the journey of an athlete

overcoming challenges, use uplifting and motivational music during B-roll sequences capturing training and achievements. This enhances the emotional narrative.

***

And there you have it, Docie-warriors – the essentials of B-roll, demystified and laid bare for you to wield like a true cinematic warrior. As we conclude this chapter, remember that B-roll isn't just supplementary; it's the unsung hero, the sidekick that elevates your documentary into a visual symphony.

Throughout this chapter, we've adhered to a practical approach – no fancy language, just simple tips and tricks to make your visuals pop. Like a true warrior you've honed your B-roll skills, turning them into a potent storytelling tool.

As you embark on your cinematic journey, armed with the knowledge acquired here, remember that B-roll isn't meant to steal the spotlight; it's the subtle force that enhances your storytelling. It's the panoramic shot that sets the stage, the macro close-up that reveals hidden worlds, and the rhythmic pacing that guides your audience through the narrative rhythm.

Exercise:

1. Combine the Essential and Advanced: Choose a scene from your documentary and plan B-roll footage that utilizes both foundational techniques (composition, framing, sound design) and advanced approaches (time-lapses, close-ups, symbolism). Analyze how your combined B-

roll approach contributes to the scene's narrative impact and emotional resonance.

2. Embrace a Creative Challenge: Pick a theme or emotion from your documentary and try capturing B-roll visuals that embody it abstractly. Use unconventional angles, unexpected juxtapositions, or symbolic elements to challenge viewers' interpretations and add layers of meaning.

3. Collaborate and Learn: Discuss B-roll challenges and solutions with the documentary community. Share your successes, resourcefulness hacks, and logistical hurdles overcome. Learn from others' experiences and expand your solo B-roll toolkit with innovative strategies.

4. Analyze B-Roll Masters: Watch documentaries renowned for their B-roll usage. Identify how the filmmakers utilize advanced techniques, sound design, and editing to create B-roll that seamlessly integrates with the narrative and elevates the overall documentary experience.

5. Edit with Intention: Integrate your captured B-roll footage into your documentary, experiment with different sequences and transitions, and use sound design to create a cohesive and impactful visual narrative. Remember, every shot should count, contributing to the emotional and thematic core of your story.

9

DAY 9

Post Production Excellence

Ah, post-production—the forge where the raw spirit of footage undergoes a transformation into the heartbeat of cinematic magic.

. Your raw video is the big playground, and you get to decide how everything fits together to tell a cool story. Editing is like using a special sword to cut out boring parts, set the rhythm, and make a story that sounds good.

The post-production steps are like being in a secret club, where you learn how to make your movie awesome. You're the solo hero, and you use your special tools to make your documentary into something really special. It's not just about cutting and pasting; it's about turning everyday shots into something really cool.

So, put on your warrior gear and lets learn the secrets, try out the tricks, and let our warrior spirits make your solo documentary into a movie that people will love.

The Big Picture: Stages of Your Solo Post-Production Workflow:

ADOBE CREATIVE CLOUD:

For this section, we had to pick a software to use in post and to start off, nothing beats Adobe Creative Cloud (in my humble opinion). There are plenty of other softwares and tutorials to boot, but I have found that master the creative cloud provides you with a gateway to a world of creative possibilities. At the core lies Adobe Premiere Pro—an editing powerhouse available on both Mac OS and Windows. To embark on your solo documentary post-production journey, let's initiate with Adobe Creative Cloud:
  GETTING STARTED:

Subscription:

  - Visit the Adobe Creative Cloud website to embark on your creative journey. Choose a subscription plan that suits your needs, such as All Apps for a comprehensive suite.
  - Following subscription, create an Adobe ID and complete the subscription process

Installation:

  - Download the Creative Cloud application from Adobe's official site and run the installer, following the on-screen instructions.
  - Open Creative Cloud, sign in with your Adobe ID, and install Adobe Premiere Pro from the available applications.

Getting Familiar:

- Open Adobe Premiere Pro to explore the intuitive workspace. Familiarize yourself with essential panels like Project, Timeline, and Effects.
- Now, equipped with Adobe Creative Cloud, let's delve into the stages of post-production:

INGESTION AND ORGANIZATION:

The ingestion and organization stage sets the groundwork for a seamless editing experience. Importing, labeling, and organizing your footage not only ensure accessibility but also lay the foundation for a well-structured and efficient editing process. The product of this stage is a neatly organized project ready for the creative journey ahead.

IMPORTING FOOTAGE:

Adobe Premiere Pro becomes your canvas as you import raw footage, breathing life into your project. Create a new project, establish your workspace, and utilize the Media Browser to seamlessly bring your clips into the Project panel.

Steps:

- Open Adobe Premiere Pro.
- Create a new project and save it to your desired location.
- Use the Media Browser to navigate to your footage.
- Select clips and drag them into the Project panel.

LABELING CLIPS

Efficient organization begins with labeling. By assigning colors or categories to your clips in the Project panel, you enhance visual clarity and streamline your editing process, allowing for swift identification of crucial elements.

Steps:

- In the Project panel, right-click on a clip.
- Choose "Label" and assign a color or category.
- This helps in visually organizing and identifying footage.

FILE STORAGE AND BACKUP

Establish a robust system for file storage and backup. Create a well-structured project folder on your computer, ensuring easy access and project integrity. Regularly save your project file and consider external drives or cloud storage for added security.

Steps For Mac OS:

1. Create a Folder Structure:

- Open Finder and navigate to the location where you want to store your documentary project.
- Right-click and select "New Folder."
- Name the folder with a clear, descriptive title for your project.

2. Save and Backup Your Project:

- Open Adobe Premiere Pro and your documentary project.
- Go to "File" in the top menu and select "Save As."
- Choose your project folder as the destination and save your project with an easily identifiable name.
- Regularly press Command ($\mathcal{H}$) + S to save incremental changes.

3. External Drives for Backup:

- Connect your external drive to your Mac.
- In Finder, locate your project folder.
- Drag and drop the entire project folder onto your external drive for a manual backup.
- Consider using Time Machine to set up automatic backups.

4. Cloud Storage for Additional Backup:

- Choose a cloud storage service (e.g., Google Drive, Dropbox).
- Install the desktop application and sign in.
- Drag your project folder into the cloud storage folder on your computer.
- Allow time for the files to sync to the cloud, providing an additional layer of backup.

Steps for Windows:

1. Create a Folder Structure:

- Open File Explorer and navigate to the location where you want to store your documentary project.
- Right-click and select "New" > "Folder."

- Name the folder appropriately for your project.

2. Save and Backup Your Project:

- Open Adobe Premiere Pro and your documentary project.
- Go to "File" in the top menu and select "Save As."
- Choose your project folder as the destination and save your project with a clear name.
- Regularly press Ctrl + S to save incremental changes.

3. External Drives for Backup:

- Connect your external drive to your PC.
- In File Explorer, locate your project folder.
- Copy and paste the entire project folder onto your external drive for manual backup.
- Set up automatic backups using built-in tools or third-party software.

4. Cloud Storage for Additional Backup:

- Choose a cloud storage service compatible with Windows (e.g., OneDrive, Google Drive).
- Install the desktop application and sign in.
- Drag your project folder into the cloud storage folder on your computer.
- Allow time for the files to sync, providing an additional layer of backup.

Tips:

- **Naming Conventions:** Use a consistent naming convention for folders and files to enhance organization.
- **Scheduled Backups:** Set reminders to perform regular backups, ensuring the most recent version is safeguarded.
- **Version Control:** If making major changes, consider creating different project versions for easy reference and retrieval.

ROUGH CUT ASSEMBLY:

In the Rough Cut Assembly stage, your documentary starts taking shape. It's the canvas where you experiment with the arrangement of your narrative elements, allowing for flexibility and refinement. The product is an evolving narrative structure that forms the backbone of your documentary.

BASIC STRUCTURE:

Transitioning into the realm of storytelling, the Rough Cut Assembly stage is where you start piecing together the basic structure of your documentary. Utilize Adobe Premiere Pro's intuitive tools to arrange interviews, B-roll footage, and narration, creating a sequence that logically flows and sets the foundation for your narrative.

Steps:

- Drag selected clips from the Project panel to the Timeline.

- Use the Razor tool (C) to cut clips and the Selection tool (V) to arrange them.
- Experiment with the basic flow of your narrative.

ITERATION AND REFINEMENT:

Embrace iteration and refinement as you experiment with the arrangement of your visual elements. The Rough Cut Assembly is a dynamic process, allowing you to iterate, refine, and iterate again until you achieve a compelling and logical sequence.

Steps:

- Embrace the iterative process; it's okay to rearrange and modify.
- Refine the sequence until you achieve a logical and compelling story flow.

FINE TUNING THE NARRATIVE

As you fine-tune the narrative, the focus shifts to the intricacies of pacing and continuity. This stage demands critical analysis, a keen eye for storytelling effectiveness, and a commitment to ensuring a seamless viewer experience. Your product is a refined narrative structure that sets the stage for impactful storytelling.

PACING AND TRIMMING:

Fine-tuning the narrative involves a meticulous approach to pacing and trimming. Zoom into the Timeline, utilize tools like the Ripple Edit tool, and trim unnecessary footage to ensure a balanced and engaging pace. Adjusting the timing of clips is pivotal for narrative fluidity.

Steps:

- Zoom into the Timeline for a detailed view.
- Use the Ripple Edit tool (B) to trim clips without leaving gaps.
- Adjust pacing by dragging the ends of clips.

CONTINUITY CHECK:

Ensuring smooth transitions between scenes becomes a priority. Utilize markers to note areas requiring attention, ensuring that your documentary maintains continuity and captivates the viewer without disruptions.

Steps:

- Ensure smooth transitions between clips.
- Use the Markers (M) to note areas needing attention.

Using Keyframes:

Keyframes are like magic markers that help you make things happen in your video over time. Whether you want to smoothly adjust effects, control how visible or see-through something is, or even move elements around the screen, keyframes are your go-to tool. It's like telling your video, "Hey, change like this at this moment!" without having to manually do it for every frame. With keyframes, you're in control, creating dynamic and eye-catching changes in your video that captivate your audience.

Steps:

Select the Clip or Effect:

- In the timeline, select the clip or effect you want to animate with keyframes.

Go to the Effect Controls Panel:

- Locate the Effect Controls panel. If it's not visible, go to "Window" in the top menu and select "Effect Controls."

Identify the Property to Animate:

- In the Effect Controls panel, find the property you want to animate (e.g., Position, Scale, Opacity).

Set the Initial Keyframe:

- Move the playhead to the point where you want the animation to begin.
- Click the stopwatch icon next to the property to set the initial keyframe.

Move the Playhead:

- Move the playhead to the point where you want the animation to end.

Adjust the Property:

- Change the value of the property (e.g., move the clip, adjust opacity) to the desired end state.

Automatically Creates Keyframes:

- Premiere Pro automatically creates keyframes between the initial and final positions, creating a smooth animation.

Tips:

Fine-Tuning Keyframes:

- To fine-tune keyframes, you can manually adjust their positions in the Effect Controls panel.

ENHANCING WITH AUDIO

Solid audio has the potential to elevate your documentary to world-class status. Enhance your documentary by introducing a layer of auditory richness. Sound design, impactful effects, and carefully selected music contribute to the overall emotional resonance of your narrative. What you end up with is an immersive auditory experience that complements and heightens your visual storytelling.

SOUND DESIGN:

Enter the world of sound design, where you breathe life into your documentary. Utilize Adobe Premiere Pro's Audio Mixer panel to import additional audio elements, balancing levels for a harmonious blend.

Steps:

- Import additional audio elements into the Project panel.
- Drag them onto separate audio tracks in the Timeline.
- navigate to the "windows" drop down menu and activate essential sound (if not already active
- Use essential sound to further enhance your audio clips by selecting the audio type, selecting appropriate presents and modifying them as you see fit.
- Use the Audio Mixer panel to balance levels.

IMPACTFUL SOUND EFFECTS (SFX):

Enhance key moments by integrating impactful sound effects. Whether sourced or created, these audio elements become integral in creating an emotional landscape that resonates with your narrative.

Steps:

- Search for or create sound effects. There are many online platforms full of sound effects for download. Make sure to

give credit where the platform requires you to.
- Mark your SFX in Essential Sound
- Align them with key moments in your film.

MUSIC:

Integrate music thoughtfully, adjusting volume levels and utilizing keyframes for gradual changes. Music becomes a powerful tool in underscoring the emotional arc of your documentary, enhancing its overall impact.

Steps:

- Import music tracks.
- Once again, Essential Sound can be used to enhance the music or even have it duck against dialogue an never overpower any voices in your timeline
- Adjust volume levels and use keyframes for gradual changes.
- Ensure music complements your narrative's emotional arc.

COLOR GRADING AND VISUAL IDENTITY:

COLOR GRADING:

Enter the realm of visual aesthetics with color grading. The Lumetri Color panel in Adobe Premiere Pro becomes your palette, allowing you to experiment with color palettes,
   Steps:

Access the Lumetri Color Panel:

- In the top menu, go to "Window" and select "Lumetri Color" to open the panel.
- It typically appears in the workspace as a separate tab.

Color Correction:

- Begin with basic color correction if necessary.
- Adjust exposure, contrast, highlights, shadows, whites, and blacks under the "Basic Correction" section.

Experiment with Presets:

- Explore the "Creative" section for preset looks that match your documentary's tone.
- Hover over presets to preview their impact before applying.

Manual Adjustments:

- For more control, navigate to the "Color Wheels & Match" section.
- Adjust color temperature, tint, and saturation manually for specific shots.

Visual Style:

- Create a consistent visual style by adjusting the "Creative" settings.
- Tweak contrast, clarity, vibrance, and saturation to achieve a cohesive look.

Tips:

Use Adjustment Layers:

- Apply color grading to an adjustment layer to affect multiple clips simultaneously.
- Right-click in the Project Panel.
- Choose "New Item" and then select "Adjustment Layer."
- drag your Adjustment Layer to your timeline and stretch it over the clips you want to affect.

Keyframes for Dynamic Changes:

- Use keyframes for dynamic changes in color over time.

Referencing Still Frames:

- Utilize the "Reference Monitor" to analyze color changes in still frames.

Monitor Calibration:

- Ensure your monitor is calibrated for accurate color representation.

Save Presets:

Save your custom color grading settings as presets for future use.

FINAL TOUCHES AND POLISHING:

Final Touches and Polishing in Adobe Premiere Pro transform your documentary into a visually appealing and professional presentation. We will cover creating text, incorporating graphics, refining timing, and preparing for export to ensure your documentary is a polished masterpiece, ready to captivate your audience.

TITLES:

Now, lets focus on creating professional and visually appealing text elements for your documentary using Adobe Premiere Pro's Text Tool to add textual elements that complement your storytelling.

Steps:

Accessing the Text Tool:

- Locate the "Type Tool" in the toolbar (shortcut: T).

Adding a Text Layer:

- Click on the Program Monitor to create a new text layer.

Essential Graphics:

- navigate to the "Windows" panel and make sure "Essential Graphics" is active.
- navigate to Essential Graphics.

Entering Text:

- Type your title or credits, adjusting font, size, and style from the Essential Graphics panel.

Fine-Tuning:

- Customize text properties directly in the Program Monitor or the Essential Graphics panel.

GRAPHICS:

Time to learn how to enhance the visual appeal of your documentary with various graphic elements. Learn the art of importing graphics, utilizing preset graphic options within the Essential Graphics panel, and even downloading and customizing templates to elevate the overall aesthetics of your project.

Steps:

Importing Graphics:

- Navigate to File > Import to bring in your graphic files. Drag them to the timeline.

Positioning Graphics:

- Use the Selection Tool (shortcut: V) to adjust the position, size, and rotation of graphics.

Using Preset Graphics:

- Explore Adobe Premiere Pro's Essential Graphics panel for preset titles, lower thirds, and other graphic elements. Drag and drop them onto your timeline.

Downloading and Importing Templates:

- Browse online marketplaces or Adobe Stock for Premiere Pro graphic templates. Download and import them into your project.

Customizing Templates:

- Edit imported templates in the Essential Graphics panel. Modify text, colors, and other parameters to suit your documentary's style.

FLOW, TIMING & PACING:

Lets dive into the intricate process of refining your documentary for seamless viewing. From scrubbing through the timeline to adjusting timing and incorporating transitions and effects, this section covers the nuances of fine-tuning your film's flow, ensuring a captivating and well-paced viewing experience.

Steps:

Timeline Scrubbing:

- Scrub through the timeline to review the entire film. Check for continuity, smooth transitions, and logical flow.

Timing Adjustments:

- Use the razor tool (shortcut: C) for precise cuts. Adjust clip durations to refine timing and pacing.

Adding Transitions:

- Navigate to the effects panel (normally in the same screen section as your project panel)
- Enhance flow with transitions from the Effects panel. Experiment with different transition styles.

Applying Effects:

- Experiment with effects to add polish. Consider color correction, stabilization, or other visual enhancements.

EXPORT:

The "Export" subsection explores the crucial steps of preparing your documentary for professional output. Lets ensure that your documentary is ready for sharing on various platforms.

Steps:

Accessing Export Options:

- Navigate to File > Export > Media to open the Export Settings window (or ctrl/cmd M).

Choosing Format and Preset:

- Select the desired format from the dropdown menu. Use presets for common outputs (e.g., H.264 for online sharing).

Fine-Tuning Settings:

- Adjust resolution, bitrate, and codec settings. Utilize the Queue button for additional control.
- If you aren't sure, select a preset based on your needs (e.g. Youtube 4k)

Saving and Exporting:

- Choose a destination and click Export. Premiere Pro will render your project into a final video ready for sharing.

Conquering Solo Post-Production Challenges:

Staying Organized: Develop a system that works for you. Utilize software tools, label files clearly, and back up your footage regularly to avoid technical headaches and lost edits.

Overcoming Technical Hurdles: Learn basic troubleshooting techniques for software glitches, hardware issues, and data loss. Consider online tutorials or forums to solve technical challenges you encounter.

Managing Time and Resources: Prioritize tasks, set realistic deadlines, and utilize available resources like online libraries, stock footage, or royalty-free music to supplement your content.

Maintaining Objectivity: Take breaks from editing regularly. Seek feedback from trusted others to stay fresh and identify areas for improvement. Avoid falling in love with every cut and remain open to constructive criticism. This part will often hurt, but your priority is making a beautiful docie and constructive criticism goes a long way in ensuring that.

Solo Post-Production Tools and Resources:

Editing Software: Choose software that fits your skill level and budget. Popular options include Adobe Premiere Pro, Final Cut Pro, and DaVinci Resolve. Free or open-source software like OpenShot are also available for beginners. In this section we covered Premiere Pro because that is my personal favorite, but feel free to find a software you feel truly comfortable with,

Online Tutorials and Resources: Take advantage of online tutorials, webinars, and workshops to learn specific editing techniques, sound design basics, and color grading workflows. This book is a fantastic resource for learning and guiding yourself through the process of creating a documentary, but its always good to supplement even the best lessons with a variety of additional educational resources.

Community and Collaboration: Seek support from online communities of solo documentarians. Share your challenges, learn from others' experiences, and exchange valuable advice. Few things are better than the advise of a season docie-warrior.

***

You seem to be getting more comfortable in your skill docie warrior, this is great. you have come far since we began your training. Your skills in post-production are now honed and you stand strong, capable of great feats of editing. Each post-production step is a move in a dance, a strategic choice that transforms colors, adds sounds that resonate, and breathes life into visuals. From perfecting colors to evoking emotions through sound, we uncovered the secrets, tested out the tricks, and let our warrior spirits guide our solo documentary into a film that we are proud of.

As we conclude this chapter, let the lessons learned in post-production be etched into the core of your Docie-warrior identity. This cinematic journey is not merely about crafting a film; it's about channeling the essence of your story, infusing it with emotion, and presenting it to the world as a testament to the artistry of a true cinematic warrior.

Exercise:

1. Outline your post-production workflow: Sketch out a timeline for each stage, incorporating file organization, editing phases, and audio/visual enhancements. This plan will keep

you focused and motivated throughout the process.

2. Practice editing: Assemble a short sequences, utilize different cuts and transitions, and explore pacing variations. Learn the basics of sound mixing and color grading to enhance your narrative impact. Try creating a bright colorful color grade and then create a dark gloomy color grade. compare and contrast the two.

3. Seek feedback: Share your rough cuts with trusted friends, family, or fellow documentarians. Constructive criticism can help you identify areas for improvement and refine your storytelling.

4. Explore online resources: Check out tutorials on your chosen editing software, sound design techniques, and color grading basics. Learn from professional post-production experts and discover valuable tips for solo filmmakers.

5. Join a community: Connect with other solo documentarians online or in local groups. Share your challenges, celebrate successes, and learn from each other's experiences to navigate the post-production journey together.

Remember: Post-production is an iterative process. Don't be afraid to experiment, refine, and embrace the creative journey. With dedication, resourcefulness, and a passion for storytelling, you can transform your raw footage into a polished and captivating solo documentary that leaves a lasting impact.

10

DAY 10

Distribution - Expanded Edition: Unleashing Your Solo Documentary to the World

Its your final day docie warrior!!! Today, we'll delve deeper into the vibrant world of solo documentary distribution, empowering you actionable tips to share your film with the world.

Imagine this as the moment your film spreads its wings and becomes a vibrant force in the storytelling world. We're not just talking about sharing a documentary; we're talking about sharing your sacred art. So, buckle up, Docie Warrior! It's time to celebrate the journey, face any challenges with confidence, and step into the exciting world of solo documentary distribution.

Essential Elements for Documentary Distribution

SYNOPSIS:

A synopsis is a concise, compelling written summary that displays the central theme, story, and significant elements of your documentary. It is a powerful marketing tool that provides a quick glimpse into your film's essence, enticing potential viewers and partners. The goal is to generate interest, spark curiosity, and prompt further exploration of your documentary, encouraging distribution platforms to take a closer look.

Example:

Synopsis: "Pinning Unity"

In the whimsical documentary "Pinning Unity," director Taku Chimu uncovers the surprising depth behind the commonplace thumbtack, revealing its role as an unassuming yet crucial element in the tapestry of society. As the narrative unfolds, viewers are invited on a journey into the lives of diverse individuals, each connected by the humble thumbtack.

"Pinning Unity" delves into the subtle yet impactful ways thumb-tacks contribute to societal cohesion. From family bulletin boards to bustling office spaces, this often-overlooked object becomes a metaphor for connection and communication. Through intimate interviews, playful animations, and unexpected encounters, the documentary explores the multifaceted roles of thumbtacks in daily life.

The film's charm lies in its ability to spotlight the unnoticed threads that bind us together. Whether holding up cherished memories or securing essential documents, the thumbtack emerges as a silent hero, fostering unity in shared spaces. With humor and curiosity, Emma Green challenges viewers to reconsider the overlooked elements that shape our collective existence.

"Pinning Unity" is not merely a documentary about office supplies; it's a celebration of the small, often unnoticed, elements that weave the intricate tapestry of our interconnected lives. Join Emma Green on a quirky and insightful exploration that transforms the way we perceive thumbtacks, revealing the threads of connection they represent in our shared human experience. This documentary promises a delightful and thought–provoking journey, prompting audiences to see the world—and thumbtacks—in a new light.

How to create:

1. Begin with a strong hook that captures the essence of your film.
2. Introduce main characters and the central conflict or theme.
3. Conclude with a teaser or cliffhanger to generate interest.

Practical Steps:

1. Keep it concise, ideally under 300 words.
2. Highlight unique aspects that make your documentary stand out.
3. Tailor it for different platforms and audiences.

DIRECTOR'S STATEMENT:

The director's statement is a personal narrative from the director, offering insights into the motivation, vision, and creative decisions behind the documentary. It provides a deeper understanding of the filmmaker's perspective, fostering a connection with potential collaborators, distributors, and viewers. The goal is to convey authenticity, passion, and a unique perspective, establishing a compelling context for your documentary and enhancing its marketability.

Example:

Director's Statement: "Pinning Unity"

In the creation of "Pinning Unity," my goal was to illuminate the extraordinary narratives concealed within the ordinary. The humble thumbtack, often dismissed as a trivial object, became the lens through which I explored the profound connections that underpin our daily lives. This documentary is an ode to the unseen threads that weave the fabric of our shared human experience.

As a director, I was drawn to the challenge of uncovering significance in the seemingly mundane. The decision to focus on the thumbtack was not just a playful choice but a deliberate attempt to reveal the poetry hidden within the ordinary artifacts that punctuate our lives. Through a blend of humor, curiosity, and a touch of whimsy, "Pinning Unity" invites viewers to reimagine the role of these unassuming tools in our shared spaces.

The documentary unfolds as a journey of discovery, traversing diverse environments and meeting individuals whose lives are subtly influenced by thumbtacks. From the family bulletin board to the bustling office, each setting becomes a microcosm of the broader human experience. The interviews, animations, and encounters captured on film serve to illuminate the multifaceted roles of thumbtacks as symbols of connection, memory, and unity.

In "Pinning Unity," I sought to challenge preconceptions and prompt reflection on the overlooked elements that silently bind us together. Through this exploration, I aimed to offer a fresh perspective on the significance of everyday objects, encouraging audiences to find beauty and meaning in the small, often unnoticed, details of life.

-Taku Chimu

How to create:

1. Reflect on why you chose this topic and your personal connection.
2. Discuss the creative decisions made during filming and post-production.
3. Express the impact you hope the documentary will have.

Practical Steps:

1. Be genuine and authentic in your tone.
2. Keep it focused and concise, around 500 words.
3. Tailor it to align with the tone and themes of your documentary.

TRAILER:

A trailer is a visually captivating preview, offering a dynamic representation of your documentary, designed to generate excitement and anticipation. It serves as a powerful marketing tool, creating a strong first impression and compelling potential viewers to seek out the full documentary. The goal is to showcase the documentary's highlights, evoke curiosity, and leave a memorable impact, motivating distributors, festivals, and viewers to engage with the full film.

How to create:

1. Include captivating snippets showcasing the documentary's visuals.
2. Introduce key characters and highlight dramatic or emotional moments.
3. Use music and narration to set the tone.

Practical Steps:

1. Aim for a duration of 1–2 minutes.
2. Create multiple versions for different platforms.
3. Optimize for online viewing, considering mobile users

POSTER:

A poster is an image that serves as a visual representation of your documentary, combining imagery and information to capture attention and communicate key details. It acts as a visual hook, drawing in potential viewers and conveying essential information about the documentary at a glance. The goal is to create a visually appealing and informative promotional tool that stands out, leaving a lasting impression and enticing viewers to explore further.

Example:

How to create:

- Use striking imagery relevant to your documentary's theme.

- Include essential details: title, tagline, credits, and release information.
- Maintain a consistent visual style with your film.

Practical Steps:

- Prioritize clarity and simplicity.
- Utilize high-resolution images for print and online promotion.
- Test different designs for audience feedback.

Beyond the Mainstream: Unconventional Distribution Avenues:

As a solo or small documentarian, reaching diverse audiences involves exploring a variety of distribution methods. Each approach not only broadens your film's exposure but also engages communities expands your network and increases your potential to tackle bigger projects in the future. Let's delve into diverse distribution strategies tailored for docie warriors like us:

MICRO-CINEMAS AND INDEPENDENT SCREENINGS

For an intimate viewing experience and community dialogue, partner with local arthouse cinemas or independent screening spaces. This approach allows you to connect with your audience on a personal level and also meet other creators like yourself whose passion and inspirations may allow you to expand your scope and also broaden your knowledge.

How to: Research local arthouse cinemas or independent screening spaces in your community. Reach out to them, expressing your interest in hosting a screening.

Practical Insight: Prepare a compelling pitch highlighting the uniqueness of your documentary. Offer collaboration ideas, such as post-screening discussions or Q&A sessions, to enhance the viewer experience.

.

FILM FESTIVALS WITH A NICHE FOCUS

Discovering festivals that align with your documentary's theme or genre is a powerful way to reach targeted audiences and industry professionals. Festivals also lead to some notable accolades as winning festivals or even getting selected to screen would be both validating on your part and a sure fire way to impress any potential investors in your future work.

How to: Utilize platforms like **FilmFreeway** to discover festivals aligning with your documentary's theme or genre. Prepare a well-crafted submission package, including a captivating synopsis, posters (**Canva** is a powerful ally), director's statement and a trailer.

Practical Insight: Tailor your submission to showcase what makes your documentary stand out. Highlight any awards or

recognition, creating a compelling case for festival program-
mers.

EDUCATIONAL SCREENINGS AND CURRICULUM INTEGRATION

Extend your documentary's impact by reaching educational institutions. Your documentary could become part of courses or workshops, offering educational value and training future docie warriors. Just as you have received powerful knowledge, you mayfind great purpose (and benefit) in imparting it.

How to: Identify universities, high schools, or educational organizations relevant to your documentary. Reach out to educators or program coordinators, proposing your film for potential integration.

Practical Insight Develop educational materials and discussion guides to accompany your documentary. Emphasize the edu-cational value your film brings to students.

COMMUNITY CENTERS AND NGOs

Collaborate with community organizations and non-profits aligned with your documentary's social impact goals. by organizing screenings and discussions in community centers or through NGO partnerships, you will amplify the societal dialogue sparked by your documentary and put in place the foundation upon which you can inspire true change through your art.

How to: Connect with local community centers or non-profits aligned with your documentary's themes. Propose collaboration for screenings or events.

Practical Insight: Tailor your outreach to emphasize the community impact of your documentary. Showcase how the film aligns with the mission and goals of the organizations you approach.

SOCIAL MEDIA AND ONLINE COMMUNITIES

Harness the power of online platforms to organically reach engaged audiences. Utilize Facebook groups, Reddit communities, or niche platforms relevant to your film's topic to reach passionate audiences and fellow docie-warriors. Movements and fan bases are built on social platforms, so distributing directly to those platforms could be exactly what your documentary needs to hit the big time.

How to: **Create a YouTube channel and upload your video.** Identify relevant Facebook groups, Reddit communities, or niche platforms related to your documentary's topic and promote your documentary. consider posting directly to these platforms as well and promoting using your trailer and poster. Engage with the community by sharing content, initiating discussions, and building anticipation.

Practical Insight: Create shareable content such as behind-the-scenes footage, exclusive interviews, or teaser clips to generate buzz within online communities.

VIRTUAL REALITY AND IMMERSIVE EXPERIENCES

Explore cutting-edge distribution methods by considering VR platforms and interactive content. Virtual reality provides a unique and engaging way for audiences to experience your documentary.

How to: Explore VR platforms that align with your documentary's narrative. Collaborate with VR creators or platforms to adapt your content for immersive experiences.

Practical Insight: Offer a teaser or sample of your VR content to showcase the unique and engaging aspects of your documentary. Create a buzz by emphasizing the innovative nature of your distribution approach.

Diverse distribution opens doors to varied audiences, and as a solo documentarian, these methods empower you to share your story in meaningful ways. Each approach is a unique avenue for connecting with communities, fostering dialogue, and making a lasting impact. Tailor your distribution strategy to your documentary's narrative, and let these diverse channels amplify the reach of your cinematic creation.

-

Conquering Distribution Challenges as a Solo Filmmaker

The distribution phase is often tough to predict and is akin to uncharted territory. In this section, we will map the complex landscape that often accompanies solo distribution, offering a comprehensive guide to overcoming challenges and maximizing the reach of your documentary.

With each distribution challenge explored, you'll gain practical insights and actionable strategies to amplify your documentary's impact.

LIMITED RESOURCES AND MARKETING BUDGETS:

Facing the constraints of limited resources and modest marketing budgets is a common challenge for solo filmmakers. However, creativity can be a powerful ally in overcoming these hurdles. Collaborate with other filmmakers to pool resources and engage in cross-promotion, broadening your reach through shared audiences. Leverage free online marketing tools, from social media platforms to email campaigns, to maximize your outreach without straining your budget. The organic growth potential on platforms like Instagram, Twitter, and Facebook can be harnessed by crafting compelling content and actively engaging with your audience. Think outside the box; consider unconventional partnerships or grassroots initiatives that align with your documentary's themes, making the most of every available resource.

How To:

1. **Partner Collaboratively:** Identify fellow filmmakers or creators whose content aligns with yours. Propose collaborative projects to pool resources and share audiences.
2. **Utilize Free Tools:** Leverage online platforms like Canva for graphic design, Mailchimp for email campaigns, and Hootsuite for social media scheduling, all of which offer free versions.
3. **Engage Organically:** Actively participate in social media conversations, respond to comments, and encourage discussions. Authentic engagement often leads to increased visibility.

Practical Insights: Collaborating with others not only expands your reach but also fosters a sense of community. Utilize user-generated content and testimonials in your marketing efforts to build credibility.

RIGHTS MANAGEMENT AND LEGAL INTRICACIES:

Navigating the complex legal landscape of distribution requires a solid understanding of rights management and legal intricacies. Seeking legal advice on distribution contracts is crucial to ensure your rights are protected and that you retain control over your film's intellectual property. Delve into the specifics of platform-specific terms and conditions before committing to any distribution avenue, preventing potential conflicts in the future. Keeping yourself informed about copyright laws and industry standards is an ongoing process, and utilizing legal tools tailored for filmmakers can be beneficial. By staying vigilant about your film's legal aspects, you empower yourself to make informed decisions and safeguard your creative work throughout the distribution journey.

How To:

1. **Seek Legal Counsel:** Consult with an entertainment lawyer to review distribution contracts, ensuring clarity on rights, royalties, and any potential exclusivity clauses.
2. **Read Platform Terms:** Thoroughly review the terms and conditions of any distribution platform before committing. Look for clauses related to exclusivity, revenue sharing, and ownership.
3. **Use Legal Resources:** Platforms like LegalZoom offer tailored legal services for filmmakers. Utilize these resources to understand and protect your intellectual property rights.
4. **Obtain Signed Releases:** Make sure all your documentary subjects and interviewees are on board with distributing the documentary and that they have sign releases allowing you to capture video of them and distribute it. Quick Tip: Avoid filming children unless you the express consent of their parents because it can land you in trouble in some situations.

Practical Insights: Investing in legal guidance upfront can save you from potential legal disputes down the line. Clear contractual agreements contribute to a smoother and more secure distribution experience.

REACHING INTERNATIONAL AUDIENCES:

Expanding the geographic impact of your documentary involves strategic planning to reach international audiences. Researching international film festivals aligned with your documentary's themes provides opportunities for exposure on a global scale. Explore online platforms with a worldwide reach, ensuring your film can be accessed by diverse audiences. Investigate potential foreign distribution partners who understand the cultural nuances and preferences of different regions. Building connections with individuals or organizations experienced in international distribution can open doors to new markets and foster a broader appreciation for your work.

How To:

1. **Research Film Festivals:** Explore international film festivals that align with your documentary's themes. Platforms like FilmFreeway can simplify the festival submission process.
2. **Leverage Online Platforms:** Choose streaming services with a global audience, such as Vimeo On Demand or Amazon Prime Video, to broaden your film's reach.
3. **Connect with Distributors:** Network with international distributors or sales agents who have experience in reaching diverse markets. Attend industry events or use online platforms for introductions.

Practical Insights: Understanding cultural sensitivities and preferences is crucial when aiming for international reach. Tailor your promotional materials for different regions to enhance relatability.

DATA ANALYSIS AND AUDIENCE ENGAGEMENT:

Harnessing the power of data analysis and audience engagement is crucial for refining your distribution strategy. Utilize platform analytics to gain insights into your audience demographics, viewing patterns, and engagement metrics. Understanding who your audience is and how they interact with your content enables you to tailor your outreach strategies effectively. Adapt your approach based on the data, emphasizing the aspects of your documentary that resonate most with viewers. Engaging with your audience on social media platforms fosters a sense of community, creating a dedicated fan base that can amplify your film's reach through word-of-mouth and online sharing.

How To:

1. **Utilize Platform Analytics:** Platforms like YouTube and Vimeo provide detailed analytics. Understand your audience demographics, watch time, and geographical reach.
2. **Adapt Content Strategy:** Tailor your content based on audience preferences. Emphasize themes or aspects of your documentary that resonate most with viewers.
3. **Engage on Social Media:** Actively participate in discussions, ask for feedback, and respond to comments on social media. Create a sense of community around your

documentary.

Practical Insights: Regularly analyze audience engagement data to refine your content strategy. Use insights to create targeted promotional materials for specific audience segments.

OVERCOMING TECHNICAL HURDLES:

Solo filmmakers often encounter technical hurdles when navigating the distribution landscape. Overcome these challenges by familiarizing yourself with essential platform submission requirements. Each platform may have unique specifications for video formats, resolutions, and file sizes, so staying well-informed is crucial. Be prepared to troubleshoot formatting issues promptly to ensure a smooth submission process. Stay updated on evolving distribution technologies, keeping abreast of new tools and features that can enhance your film's presentation. A proactive approach to technical aspects ensures that your documentary is not only compelling but also technically polished for a seamless viewing experience.

Exercise:

1. Map your audience journey: Identify your ideal viewer and create a visual map of their journey from discovering your film to engaging with it on a chosen platform. This

will help you tailor your distribution strategy effectively.

2. Brainstorm unconventional distribution ideas: Think outside the box! Brainstorm creative ways to reach your target audience through non-traditional platforms, partnerships, or community engagement initiatives.

3. Develop a distribution budget: Assess your financial resources and allocate funds for platform fees, marketing expenses, travel costs (festivals), and potential legal consultation.

4. Research and contact potential distributors: Explore different distribution platforms, research their target audiences and niche focus, and connect with relevant contacts to discuss your film's potential fit.

5. Design your social media strategy: Create a content calendar, identify relevant hashtags, and engage with online communities related to your film's theme to build anticipation and audience excitement.

YOU DID IT!!!!

Ten days have thundered by, warriors of the lens! We've charged through the pre-production jungle, bested editing hyenas, and emerged, sweat-slicked and grinning, with the power to weave documentaries that roar with the power and voice of the docie warrior and whisper like savanna winds. You started as raw recruits, eager but untested, but now, the warrior spirit courses through your veins.

Remember, your journey doesn't end here. The lessons learned here are your spears, honed and ready to pierce the unknown. Embrace the detours, celebrate the triumphs, and let the fire of your passion be the sun that guides your cinematic trek.

Know this, even on the shoots that will test your patience and the long nights of endless editing , you're not alone. We, your fellow tribe members, still shake our warrior rattles in your support. We believe in the tales you carry, in the magic you'll unleash.

So grab your camera, let the war cries of your inspiration echo across the Earth, and paint the world with your cinematic dreams. Remember, the biggest story of all isn't on the screen, it's the one you're writing right now, with every frame, every edit, every beat of your courageous heart.

Film on, brave storytellers, film on! And know this, the world, with ears to the ground and hearts pounding, awaits the tales you'll roar into existence.

"CONGRATULATIONS, YOU ARE NOW A FULL FLEDGED
DOCIE WARRIOR"

RESOURCES

In this section, you will find templates, examples and resources that will be useful in your journey to becoming a Docie-Warrior. Use this knowledge wisely.

Documentary Consent Form

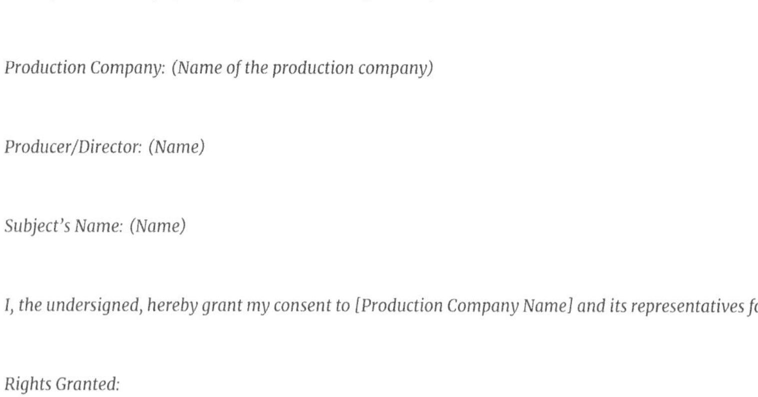

Title of Documentary: (What is your documentary called?)

Production Company: (Name of the production company)

Producer/Director: (Name)

Subject's Name: (Name)

I, the undersigned, hereby grant my consent to [Production Company Name] and its representatives fc

Rights Granted:

I understand that by signing this consent form, I grant [Production Company Name] the irrevocabl

Release and Waiver:

I release [Production Company Name], its agents, employees, contractors, and any third parties act

Understanding of Participation:

> *I understand that my participation in the Documentary is voluntary, and I have not been coerced or und*

Compensation:

> *I acknowledge that I am not entitled to any compensation, financial or otherwise, for my participation i*

Confidentiality:

> *I understand that certain information revealed during the filming of the Documentary may be sensitive*

Duration of Consent:

> *This consent is effective as of the date of my signature below and will remain in effect indefinitely.*

Governing Law:

> *This consent form shall be governed by and construed in accordance with the laws of [State/Country].*

I acknowledge that I have read and understood the terms of this consent form and agree to be bound by its

Subject's Full Name: (Who are your covering/interviewing)

Signature: (Their Signature)

Date: (The date they signed/ are signing on)

Parental/Guardian Consent (if subject is a minor): (Signature)

I, the undersigned, am the parent or legal guardian of the subject named above and hereby consent to the t

Parent/Guardian Full Name: (Name)

Signature: (Their signature)

Date: (The date they signed/ are signing on)

***

Documentary Story Outline Template

Title: [Title of the Documentary]

    Working Logline: [Brief summary capturing the essence of the documentary]

    I. Introduction

Working Title:

- *Introduce the tentative title for your documentary.*

Synopsis:

- *Provide a concise overview of the documentary's subject matter and themes.*

Logline:

- *Craft a brief logline that encapsulates the core narrative or message.*

II. Concept Development

Objective:

- *Clearly state the primary objective or goal of the documentary.*

Target Audience:

- *Identify the demographic or community you intend to engage.*

Key Message:

- *Define the central message or takeaway you want viewers to grasp.*

III. Story Structure

Act 1: Introduction to the Subject

- *Establish the context and significance of the subject.*
- *Introduce key characters, locations, or elements.*

Act 2: Exploration and Development

- *Dive into the depth of the subject, unveiling layers and complexities.*
- *Introduce challenges, conflicts, or turning points.*

Act 3: Climax and Resolution

- *Build towards a climax, resolving conflicts or presenting pivotal moments.*
- *Reinforce the central message or perspective.*

IV. Characters

Main Characters:

- *Identify the main individuals or entities driving the narrative.*
- *Provide brief character profiles.*

Supporting Characters:

- *Introduce any supporting characters contributing to the overall story.*

V. Filming Style and Techniques

Visual Style:

- *Outline the preferred visual style, such as cinematography, color palette, or use of archival footage.*

Interview Approach:

- *Specify the interview style, tone, and techniques (if applicable).*

Use of Footage:

- *Describe how archival footage, animations, or re-enactments (if any) will be incorporated.*

VI. Locations and Settings

Primary Locations:

- *Identify the main settings where the documentary will unfold.*

Symbolic Locations:

- *Highlight any locations that hold symbolic or thematic significance.*

VII. Timeline and Schedule

Filming Timeline:

- *Outline the expected timeline for shooting and production.*

Post-Production Schedule:

- *Provide an estimated schedule for editing, sound design, and finalization.*

VIII. Funding and Budgeting

Budget Overview:

- *Outline the anticipated budget, including pre-production, production, and post-production costs.*

Funding Sources:

- *Identify potential funding sources, grants, or partnerships.*

IX. Outreach and Impact

Distribution Plan:

- *Specify the distribution channels (festivals, streaming platforms, etc.).*

Impact Goals:

- *Define the desired impact on the audience or community.*

X. Conclusion

Closing Thoughts:

- *Summarize the key elements of the documentary.*

Next Steps:

- *Outline the immediate steps needed to progress from the story outline to the production phase.*

Note: *Adjust the template based on the unique requirements of your documentary and the specific nat*

$* * *$

Documentary Shot Types

Documentary Title: [Title of the Documentary]

  Date: [Date of Filming]

  Location: [Primary Filming Location]

1. Opening Shots:

- *Establishing shots of the documentary's primary location.*
- *Shots introducing the main theme or subject.*

2. Interviews:

- *Interview with [Main Subject 1].*
- *Close-up shots.*
- *Wide shots capturing the surroundings.*
- *Interview with [Main Subject 2].*
- *Focus on facial expressions and emotions.*
- *Different angles for variety.*

3. B-Roll Footage:

- *Capture footage of [Subject's daily activities].*
- *Close-ups of details (hands, facial expressions).*
- *Wide shots to show the environment.*
- *Additional B-Roll of [Subject's surroundings].*
- *Focus on significant elements or symbols.*

4. Archival Footage:

- *Integrate historical footage related to the documentary's theme.*
- *Clearly label sources and dates for reference.*

5. Narrative Sequences:

- *Film sequences illustrating key points in the narrative.*
- *Ensure a variety of shot sizes (wide, medium, close-up).*

6. Explanatory Graphics:

- *Include shots for potential graphics or animations.*
- *Plan for explanatory visuals or infographics.*

7. Cutaways:

- *Capture cutaway shots for smooth editing transitions.*
- *Focus on details or secondary elements.*

8. Behind-the-Scenes:

- *Footage of the documentary team at work.*
- *Capture candid moments and interactions.*

9. Vox Pops:

- *Short interviews with the public or experts.*
- *Gather opinions or insights on the documentary's subject.*

10. Closing Shots:

- *Final shots summarizing the documentary.*

- *Visuals that leave a lasting impression.*

11. Transition Shots:

- *Shots that can be used for scene transitions.*

- *Consider establishing shots or thematic transitions.*

12. Additional Notes:

- *Any specific shots or sequences to be discussed with the editor.*

- *Additional shots needed for specific scenes or events.*

***

Documentary Equipment Checklist Template:

Project Information:

Documentary Title:

Date:

Director:

Cinematographer:

Location(s):

Duration of Shoot:

Camera Gear:

1. *Camera:*

- *[ ] Main Camera:*

- *[ ] Backup Camera:*

2. Lenses:

- [ ] Wide-angle lens:

- [ ] Standard lens:

- [ ] Telephoto lens:

- [ ] Specialty lenses (if needed):

3. Tripod:

- [ ] Sturdy Tripod:

- [ ] Monopod (if needed):

4. Camera Batteries:

- [ ] Main Camera Batteries:

- [ ] Backup Camera Batteries:

- [ ] Battery Charger(s):

5. Memory Cards:

- [ ] Sufficient Number of Memory Cards:

- [ ] Card Reader:

6. Camera Accessories:

- [ ] Lens Filters (e.g., ND, Polarizer):

- [ ] Lens Hoods:

- [ ] Lens Cleaning Kit:

- [ ] Rain Cover:

Audio Equipment:

7. Microphones:

- [ ] Shotgun Microphone:

- [ ] Lavalier Microphones:

- [ ] Handheld Microphone:

8. Audio Recorder:

- [ ] Portable Audio Recorder:

- [ ] Backup Audio Recorder:

- [ ] External Microphone Adapter:

9. Boom Pole:

- [ ] *Extendable Boom Pole:*

- [ ] *Shock Mount:*

10. *Headphones:*

- [ ] *High-Quality Headphones:*

11. *Audio Cables:*

- [ ] *XLR Cables:*

- [ ] *Auxiliary Cables:*

Lighting Equipment:

12. *Lighting:*

- [ ] *LED Panel Lights:*

- [ ] *Portable Light Kits:*

- [ ] *Light Stands:*

- [ ] *Diffusers/Reflectors:*

13. *Batteries and Chargers:*

- [ ] *Batteries for Lights:*

- [ ] *Battery Chargers:*

14. *Portable Generator (if shooting in remote locations):*

- [ ] *Portable Power Generator:*

- [ ] *Necessary Cables:*

Support and Stabilization:

15. *Gimbal/Stabilizer:*

- [ ] *Gimbal/Stabilizer:*

- [ ] *Gimbal Batteries:*

- [ ] *Gimbal Charger:*

16. *Camera Rig:*

- [ ] *Shoulder Rig:*

- [ ] *Follow Focus System:*

- [ ] *Matte Box:*

17. *Slider/Dolly (if needed):*

- [ ] *Slider/Dolly:*

- [ ] *Tripod for Slider/Dolly:*

- [ ] *Lubricants and Cleaning Kit:*

Miscellaneous Accessories:

18. *Camera Bags/Cases:*

- [ ] *Camera Bag/Backpack:*

- [ ] *Hard Cases for Sensitive Equipment:*

19. *Power Strips and Extensions:*

- [ ] *Power Strips:*

- [ ] *Extension Cords:*

20. *Tool Kit:*

- [ ] *Basic Tools (screwdrivers, pliers, etc.):*

- [ ] *Multi-Tool:*

21. *Clamps and Mounts:*

- [ ] *Clamps and Mounting Accessories:*

- [ ] *Gaffer Tape:*

Personal Items:

22. *Production Assistant Kit:*

- [ ] *First Aid Kit:*

  [ ] *Multi Tool:*

- [ ] *Walkie-Talkies (if working with a team):*

23. *Personal Comfort:*

- [ ] *Water Bottles:*

- [ ] *Snacks:*

- [ ] *Weather-Appropriate Clothing:*

- [ ] *Umbrella/Rain Gear (if needed):*

Notes:

- [ ] *Check and charge all batteries the night before the shoot.*

- [ ] Ensure all equipment is in working condition.

- [ ] Double-check that all necessary accessories and cables are packed.

This comprehensive documentary equipment checklist provides a foundation for planning and executi

FILM WORDS AND DEFINITIONS

This Film Production Glossary is not comprehensive. There are many film terms utilized throughout the industry and this specific list only serves to give you a head start in understanding some of them:

A:

ADR (Automatic Dialogue Replacement): Re-recording dialogue in post-production.

Ambient Sound: The background noise or atmosphere in a scene.

Ambisonic Microphone: Captures sound in 360 degrees, providing a three-dimensional audio experience.

Animation: Creating moving images through successive drawings or CGI.

Aperture: Aperture refers to the opening in a camera lens through which light passes to enter the camera body.

Aps-c Sensor: Advanced Photo System type-C) a type of image sensor commonly used in digital cameras. APS-C sensors are smaller than a full-frame sensor but larger than a Micro Four Thirds sensor.

Aspect Ratio: The proportional relationship between the width and height of the frame.

B:

Backlight: Backlight refers to the illumination that comes from behind the subject and is directed toward the camera.

Blimp: In filmmaking and audio recording, a blimp is a protective housing or enclosure designed to reduce or eliminate unwanted noise, such as handling or mechanical vibrations, when using a camera or microphone.

Bokeh: The aesthetic quality of the out-of-focus areas in an image.

Boom Operator: The person responsible for positioning and operating the boom microphone.

Boom Microphone: a directional microphone mounted on the end of an extendable pole (boom pole).

Book Light: A soft, even light created by bouncing light into a reflective surface and then onto the subject.

Backlight/Rim Light: Illumination from behind the subject, separating them from the background.

Blocking: Planning and choreographing the movement of actors and the camera for a scene.

Bounce Card/Reflector: A reflective surface used to redirect and soften light on the subject.

C:

Call Sheet: A document providing details like schedule, location, and contact information for each day of shooting.

Cameo: A brief appearance or voice role of a known person in a film.

CGI (Computer-Generated Imagery): The creation of visual elements with computer software.

Chiaroscuro: A lighting technique using strong contrasts between light and dark to create a dramatic effect.

Cinematography: The art and technique of film photography and image composition.

Closed Captions: Text added to the video for the hearing impaired.

Close-up (CU):A close-up is a type of shot in filmmaking and photography that tightly frames a subject, typically focusing on their face, or a specific detail.

Color Correction: Adjusting color inconsistencies to achieve a uniform look.

Color Grading: Adjusting the colors and tones in post-production for a specific look.

Crane Shot: Elevating or lowering the camera using a crane for dynamic perspectives.

Crosscutting/Parallel Editing: Interweaving scenes from different storylines.

Cut: Transition between two shots.

Cutaway: Inserting a shot that temporarily interrupts the main action, providing context or variety.

Cucoloris: A device used to cast shadows or patterns on a subject.

D:

Dead Cat: a furry, wind-resistant cover that is placed over a microphone to minimize wind noise during outdoor recording.

Depth of Field (DOF): The range of distances in a shot where objects appear acceptably sharp.

Diegetic Sound: Sounds that originate from within the world of the film (e.g., footsteps, dialogue). Opposite is Non-Diegetic Sound (Sound addedoutside the world of the film, like a soundtrack)

Digital Intermediate (DI): The digitization and manipulation of film frames during post-production.

Diffusion: The process of scattering light to create a softer, more even illumination.

Dolly Shot: Moving the entire camera toward or away from the subject.

Dynamic Range: The difference between the darkest and lightest parts of an image.

E:

Editing: The process of assembling and refining footage to create a final film.

Extreme Close-up (ECU): A very close shot emphasizing a specific detail or emotion.

Extreme Wide (EW): A very wide shot that includes a very wide view of an environment

F:

Focal Length: The distance between the lens and the image sensor, affecting the magnification of the image. (e.g 50mm lens)

Focus: Focus refers to the clarity and sharpness of an image.

Focus Pulling: Focus pulling, also known as rack focusing, is a filmmaking technique where the camera's focus is deliberately adjusted during a shot to shift the viewer's attention from one subject or object to another.

Foley: Creating and adding sound effects in post-production.

Frame Rate: The number of frames captured per second, influencing the motion and style of the footage.

Fill Light: Supplementary light reducing shadows created by the key light.

Fine Cut: The polished version of the documentary, refined after feedback from the rough cut.

Flag: A device used to block or shape light, preventing it from hitting certain areas.

Full-Frame Sensor: A sensor equivalent to a 35mm film frame, providing a wider field of view.

G:

Gaffer: The head of the lighting department responsible for implementing the DP's lighting plan.

Gel: A colored translucent material placed in front of lights to alter their color temperature.

Gimbal: a device or stabilization system designed to keep a camera steady during movement.

Gobo: A device used to control the direction and shape of light.

Green Screen/Chroma Key: A technique for compositing visual elements in post-production.

Guerilla Filmmaking: Low-budget, often impromptu filmmaking without extensive permits or resources.

H:

High-Key Lighting: Bright and even lighting for a cheerful atmosphere.

Head Room: Head room in photography and filmmaking refers to the space between the top of a subject's head and the upper edge of the frame.

I:

In and Out Points: Marking the beginning and end of a selected portion of footage for editing.

ISO: The sensitivity of the camera's sensor to light, affecting the image's brightness.

J:

Jog Wheel: A tool used for precise frame-by-frame control during editing.

J-Cut L-Cut: Audio transitions where the sound from the next shot precedes the cut.

Jump Cut: A noticeable cut between shots, often used for stylistic effect.

K:

Key Light: The main light source, responsible for casting the dominant shadows on your subject.

L:

Lavalier Microphone: A small, clip-on microphone for hands-free audio capture.

Lens Flare: Unintended (or sometimes intentional) light reflections or artifacts caused by direct sunlight or artificial lights.

Low-Key Lighting: Creates a moody and dramatic atmosphere with pronounced shadows.

L-Cut: Audio transitions where the sound lingers after the cut.

M:

Match Cut: A cut that links two shots based on visual or auditory similarities.

Match Frame: A technique where the same frame is used in consecutive shots to maintain continuity.

Master Copy: The finalized version of the documentary used for distribution and archiving.

Medium Close-up (MCU): A shot framing the subject from the chest up.

Micro Four-Thirds Sensor: A smaller sensor size, often used in compact and mirrorless cameras.

Montage: A sequence of short shots compiled to convey a passage of time or information.

N:

Narration: The spoken commentary that provides context, explanation, or storytelling in a documentary.

Negative Fill: A lighting technique used to reduce light on one side of the subject, creating shadows and enhancing contrast in a scene.

Non-Diegetic Sound: Sounds in a film that do not originate from the world depicted on screen.

Narrative Structure: The organization and arrangement of events, scenes, and information in a documentary to create a coherent and engaging storyline

Natural Lighting: The use of available natural light sources, such as sunlight or moonlight, without additional artificial lighting.

Neutral Density Filter (ND Filter): A camera accessory that reduces the amount of light entering the lens, allowing for wider apertures or longer exposure times in bright conditions.

Noise: Unwanted visual or auditory distortion in footage. Visual noise appears as grain or speckles, while audio noise is unwanted background sounds that can degrade audio quality.

Nose Room (or Leading Room): The space in front of a

subject's face within the frame.

O:

Overexposure: The result of too much light entering the camera, causing the image to appear excessively bright or washed out.

Off-Screen: Elements or actions that occur outside the frame of the camera but are still relevant to the narrative.

On-Screen: Elements or actions that occur within the visible frame of the camera.

Opening Shot: The initial shot of a documentary or film, often chosen to establish the tone, setting, or thematic elements.

Over-the-Shoulder Shot: A shot that frames a subject from behind, revealing the back of a person's shoulder and head while focusing on what the subject is looking at.

Overhead Shot: A shot taken from above the subject, looking downward.

Offline Editing: The initial phase of the editing process where rough cuts are assembled using lower-resolution files.

On-the-Fly Shooting: Capturing footage spontaneously and without extensive planning.

Outtake: Portions of footage that are not included in the final cut of the documentary.

Over-the-Top Shot: A shot taken from an elevated position looking down on the subject or scene.

Over-the-Line Shot: A shot taken from a high angle looking down, emphasizing the separation or division between elements within the frame.

One-Take: A scene or shot captured in a single continuous recording without cuts.

Overlap Editing: A technique in editing where the end of one shot overlaps with the beginning of the next.

P:

Pan: Rotating the camera horizontally on its axis.

Pedestal: Vertical movement of the camera, raising or lowering it without changing the framing.

POV (Point of View) Shot: A shot that represents what a character is seeing, aligning the viewer with their perspective.

Practical Lighting: The use of actual light sources within the scene, like lamps or windows.

R:

Rack Focus: Shifting focus between subjects at different distances within the same shot.

Reflector: A reflector is a photographic or filmmaking accessory used to manipulate and control light. Typically made of a reflective material such as silver, gold, white, or translucent fabric.

Rendering: The process of generating the final image or sequence from the project files.

Rough Cut: The preliminary edited version of the documentary, used for initial review.

S:

Shutter Speed: The duration the camera's shutter remains open, determining the exposure time.

Shot List: A document outlining the shots needed for filming.

Shotgun Microphone (Shotgun Mic): a highly directional microphone designed to capture focused audio from a specific direction while minimizing ambient noise from other angles.

Split Edit: Separating audio and video portions of a clip to control sound and visual transitions.

Steadicam: A Steadicam is a camera stabilization system designed to provide smooth and steady footage during motion.

Storyboard: Visual representation of shots to plan the visual flow.

T:

Tilt: Rotating the camera vertically on its axis.

Tracking Shot: A shot in which the camera moves parallel to the moving subject.

Tripod: A tripod is a three-legged support structure used to stabilize and elevate a camera or other equipment.

Turndown: Adjusting the output level of a light to control its intensity.

U:

Unconventional Angles: Exploring various shooting angles to find what best suits your narrative.

Underexposure: Insufficient exposure, resulting in a dark or underlit image.

V:

VFX (Visual Effects): Computer-generated imagery or enhancements added in post-production.

Very Wide Shot (VWS): Captures a broad view of the surroundings.(The same as an Extreme Wide Shot)

Visual Style: The unique aesthetic choices that define a filmmaker's work.

W:

Wide Shot (WS): Frames the subject with a wide view of the surroundings.

Whip Pan: A quick and rapid pan movement, often used for dynamic transitions.

Wild Sound: Recording ambient sounds separate from dialogue, used in post-production for atmosphere.

Wind Shield: a protective cover or foam shield designed to reduce or eliminate wind noise when capturing audio with a microphone.

X:

XLR Cable: A type of professional audio cable with three pins, commonly used in filmmaking for connecting microphones to audio recording equipment.

X-Axis Movement: the horizontal movement of the camera, whether its moving left or right.

Y:

Y-Axis Movement: the vertical movement of the camera, whether it's tilting up or down.

Z:

Zoom In/Zoom Out (ZI/ZO): Adjusting the focal length to magnify or widen the shot.

Zoom Shot: Altering the focal length during a shot to magnify or widen the view.

About the Author

Takunda Aaron Chimutashu aka Zen ISA is an award-winning Film Director, Writer, Photographer and Pan African with a background in Engineering, Entrepreneurship and Social leadership. He is the founder and Creative Director of Immortal African Studios and co-founder and resident Film Director of award-winning production house, Visual Sensations Media. As a self-titled "Universal Creative" Zen loves to explore art in all its forms and seeks to investigate all the amazing ways art can influence and inspire our society for the better.

Having acquired an Honors Degree in Mechatronic Engineering at University and explored his passion for social leadership through volunteering at Harare City Junior Council for nearly a decade (Initially as the Junior Mayor of Harare ad subsequently as a Respectable Junior Alderman), Zen found himself still hungry to learn and expand. It was through this hunger and the subsequent journey to sate it that he found himself on film sets doing technical jobs like being set engineer or a grip. Witnessing films and TV shows being made created a deep and powerful passion for Filmmaking in him and set off his journey to becoming a full time filmmaker. Now, Zen is a Film Director, Producer, Writer, Documentarian and Photographer who has made it his mission to document and grow African stories through the visual medium.

At the core of Zen's growth were the principles of Pan-Africanism. All this combined means Zen's greatest desire is to foster the creation of a vibrant and diverse Film and art industry that spans the African continent and Diaspora, allowing artists to live off of their passion and for previously ignored stories from the African perspective to hit the mainstream.

Also by Takunda Aaron CHimutashu
(ZEN ISA)

www.ingramcontent.com/pod-product-compliance
Lightning Source LLC
Chambersburg PA
CBHW071613030726
47598CB00001B/257